Billy Fr

Tough Enough

MW00770375

Billy Franklin's
Tough Enough
The Cocaine Investigation of
United States Senator Chuck Robb

As told to

Judi Tull

Broad Bay Publishing Co., Inc.
Virginia Beach

Billy Franklin's Tough Enough is distributed by:

Hampton Roads Publishing Co., Inc.
891 Norfolk Square
Norfolk, VA 23502

Cover by Doug Hamann
Printed in the United States of America

Dedication

Billy Franklin dedicates this book to his parents,
Herman and Veva Franklin

Acknowledgements

Billy Franklin would like to thank all the people who came forward to talk with him during the course of this investigation, especially those who did so at some personal risk.

He would also like to thank the employees at Franklin Security Systems who kept the shop going, particularly Diane Heaney, Cindy Upson, Paul Timmerberg and Jay Bradshaw.

A special thank you to "Captain Charlie" and "Dutch" for struggling through those first manuscripts and finally, to his wife, Keetie, who has stood like a rock through the entire ordeal.

Billy Franklin would like to express his gratitude to the following members of his Citizens Advisory Committee:

Douglas W. Aydlette
  Aydlette-Womack Associates
Dr. Andrew T. Carrington
  Assistant Superintendant
  Virginia Beach
  Public School System
James J. DiNardo, Jr.
  Major, USMC (Ret.)
Robin E. Hill,
  M.S.W.
Vicki S. Hunt
  Real Estate Associate

Emilie B. Inman
  Deputy Clerk,
  Circuit Court
  City of Virginia Beach
Charles M. Irwin
  Captain, USN (Ret.)
H. Jack Jennings
  Insurance Broker
Sheila K. Jennings
  Real Estate Broker
Stephen G. Leonard
  HMCS,USN (Ret.)

He would also like to thank his friend and counselor, W. R. "Buster" O'Brien.

...and last but not least, to

JOHN

"I couldn't have done it without you."

Contents

Prologue

February 1989—West Texas

The silver Porsche 928 sped eastward through the Texas night. The big man gripped the steering wheel with grim determination. The tension, the misery, the sorrow of the past week filled his belly. His head ached, his eyes burned. His heart was damned near breaking.

In the dark landscape around him, it seemed as if ghosts rose up, unbidden memories, inescapable. It seemed as if he heard their voices, felt their souls stir about him.

Half a century before, the man came across these same roads heading west, through the barrenness of Texas from Seminole, Oklahoma, on toward the bounty of California. The oldest of four small children bundled up in the back of a beat up old Chevy, he was already growing accustomed to hard work being a fact of his life. On the way to the promise the West Coast held in those pre-war days, he picked cotton alongside his mother. He was five years old. "My parents," he said many years later, "didn't raise any brain surgeons or Nobel Prize winners." But the children — there was one more born in California — grew up healthy and strong-willed.

God knows, they were strong-willed. He was the third generation of a family who survived by strength. The men of the generations before him were fighters and survivors. Farmers, blacksmiths, gamblers, oilmen and cattlemen. No cowards, the man said later. No cowards.

So as he drove through the night on this trip eastward, the man remembered. Remembered his first sweet smell of orange, lemon and avocado groves — such a heady aroma for a small boy — wafting over the magnificence of San Diego County in 1941. Remembered that first trip westward, over the Laguna Mountains, in the battered old Chevy with Herman and Veva, his parents.

And he remembered, remembered — it was too close to forget, only days ago, still countable in hours, so close — remembered Veva, his mother, in her hospital bed, imploring her oldest son.

"Take me home," she begged. "Please Billy, take me home." "Mama," he said, "Mama, I can't."

The big man in the Porsche felt the tears start to sting his eyes again. He had grown so accustomed to his own strength and power in adulthood that this sudden and unexpected helplessness overwhelmed him. Powerless, he had sat beside his mother's bed, held her hand, wiped the perspiration from her brow. And he made the final decision. As the oldest, it was up to him to tell the doctor, "Yes, increase the medication to ease her pain." Even if it meant her death.

It did.

He stayed four more days. He helped bury Veva and he helped his father prepare a will. When he packed the Porsche before he left, Veva Marie Griffin Franklin's family Bible was in a box in the back.

Right beside it were the case files that had already disrupted his life and threatened to expose and derail a national political figure. There were hundreds of pages of notes from interviews, names and dates and places. A quagmire of sordid tales, loops of intrigue that folded back over themselves. Tape recordings. Newspaper clippings written by reporters who had tried to break down the same barriers he'd been butting up against. There had been litigation. Death threats. Hints of money, big money, to back down. He was enmeshed in the case, tangled up in the tentacles that seemed to reach in every direction.

He remembered how simple it had seemed, only nine months before, when he was hired to investigate the rumors that then-Governor, now U.S. Senator Charles Robb had used cocaine at parties in Virginia Beach. In the beginning, he thought it would be a quick case. Easy. Report on his findings, collect his fee.

He chuckled to himself ruefully; he remembered.

It had not been quick, and certainly not easy. This case was like a pit of quicksand instead. The further he went, the more people he talked to, the more stories he heard, the more sordid the whole mess became. Sex and drugs and politics and an entire community of men and women who knew the truth about the conduct of the man who now represented them in the United States Senate. Suddenly the rage rose up in him again. He couldn't even fly to California to his dying mother when the call reached him in Georgia because he couldn't leave the files in the car in some airport parking lot. Not after all that had already happened.

"Those bastards," he said out loud to the night air, as he slammed his hand on the steering wheel.

His health was deteriorating; his business was jeopardized. At times he feared for the safety of his wife and daughter, and his employees. He had never wavered much, but sometimes he wondered if this case was worth the pain. It would, so many times, have been easier to walk away.

But he was mad. Mad as hell that in this country — the one that he loved so much — truth could be so hard to tell.

Apparently Chuck Robb thought he could get away with illegal and immoral behavior in front of the very people he governed and that no one would ever speak the truth; to the man in the Porsche it seemed that Robb believed he lived above the law, beyond scrutiny.

In the dark of that Texas night, breathing that familiar, clear air, the big man knew that he had no choice but to persevere in his investigation. The mandate of his ancestors spurred him on; the death of his mother galvanized him. His lifelong belief in truth and democracy goaded him to complete what he had begun.

A private chapter of Bill Franklin's life had just ended with the death of his beloved mother. A very public chapter was about to begin. He pushed his foot hard on the accelerator and the Porsche jumped. Bill Franklin was going to finish what he started.

Chapter One

The Case and The Client

"Charles Robb is no Virginia gentleman."
Dr. Lewis Williams, Richmond, Va., physician

Bill Franklin started to receive the first telephone calls from friends and business associates in mid-May 1988. Someone, they said, was calling around town asking about him. The man was asking about Franklin's reputation, his credentials, his background. An out-of-towner insisting on anonymity, the stranger said he needed to have a very sensitive and confidential investigation undertaken, and he was looking for the right man to do it.

It was likely that Bill Franklin's name would come up as the right man. His reputation as an investigator, polygraph expert and crime-solver spanned the nation by then. Calls from the Deep South, the West Coast, up north: nothing was unusual, nothing was unexpected, and virtually every case was do-able.

None of the people who received those first inquiring telephone calls thought it unusual for a prospective client to call around asking about an investigator. Police departments and attorneys are accustomed to these calls. It's the kind of thing a smart client does.

At last, Dr. Lewis Williams, a physician from Richmond, called Franklin directly. The men arranged a meeting at the end of May at the Holiday Inn in Hampton, just across the James River from Norfolk.

Bill Franklin didn't know Williams, had never heard of him. Older, soft-spoken, an obstetrician and gynecologist, Dr. Williams was slightly built, his hair softly silvered by the years, with fine, delicate hands; he was dressed casually but impeccably in slacks and an open-collar shirt. His southern accent was not pronounced, not the heavy drawl of Georgia but rather the near-British phrasing, tone and lilt that is so often associated with "Old Virginia."

After very few pleasantries, Dr. Williams got right to the point.

"Have you heard the rumors about Chuck Robb in Virginia Beach?" he asked Franklin.

"Which ones?" Franklin asked, knowing that there were many. "The women. The drugs. His friends," Williams said. "I've heard them," Franklin replied.

You would have to have been deaf, blind or dead to be in Virginia Beach and not have heard them, Franklin thought to himself.

"I want to hire you to investigate the rumors. And Robb." "I think it's all bullshit," Bill Franklin said.

The older man blinked.

"Robb couldn't possibly be so stupid as to get involved in drugs," Franklin continued. "The women, maybe. But I'm not interested in doing any investigation on a former governor's extramarital affairs."

Williams nodded his head in understanding.

"But the drugs," he said. "Will you look into that? I need to know once and for all whether or not they're true."

"Why?" Franklin shot back.

"I am something of an amateur historian," Williams replied. "It's been a lifelong interest. I'm writing a book about the governors of Virginia.

"Virginia has a love affair with her governors. The position carries with it so much admiration, respect and honor. The governor almost ought to be referred to as His Excellency. It's a sacred office.

"This man," Williams went on, referring to Robb with a dismissive wave of his hand, "here comes this flash from nowhere, he marries a president's daughter, and zoom! It's straight toward the top.

"And the stories! They were everywhere. It was an embarrassment to the Commonwealth. I resent any governor behaving this way. If even a little of it is true, I'm personally affronted."

He paused, thinking, as if trying even harder to explain how one who held this Commonwealth, its history and its future so dear to his heart, would feel. The words came to him at last. "Charles Robb," he said emphatically, "is no Virginia gentlemen."

Franklin listened politely during that first meeting, but felt impatient.

"I'm no fool. Robb's running for the Senate in November. Is this about that?"

"No," Williams said, and added that he believed Robb was a sure winner in the upcoming election. It was, he explained, the other, larger future that he was worried about.

"There is no way this man should ever be president of the United States," he said.

He then requested anonymity from Franklin, which he was assured of, and the men reached an agreement that Williams would receive no information until Franklin had completed his investigation.

Bill Franklin's mind was racing. It wasn't unusual for a client to insist on anonymity, but they almost always wanted verbal reports as an investigation unfolds. He assessed his own beliefs in those few moments.

Robb and cocaine. "It couldn't possibly be," he thought to himself. He'd heard the rumors for years; the Beach had been rife with them. Parties, coke whores, prostitutes, lines of coke that disappeared up lots and lots of noses. The in-crowd of high rollers had the money, they had the time, they had the inclination. Some of them had gone to jail already, caught in a federal drug investigation that had shaken the Virginia Beach community to its roots.

And he had heard that Robb was there, in the thick of it. Franklin was incredulous. He couldn't believe that a sitting governor would actually use cocaine at all, much less in full view of scores of others. "Unadulterated bullshit" were the words that came to mind.

Franklin mentally assessed this investigation. His years of experience told him this: "It will be quick. You'll prove the rumors wrong. You'll make some money at it."

"I'll do it," Franklin told his newest client. "My fee will be $100 an hour plus incidental expenses. I'll need a retainer of $2,500.00."

Dr. Williams paid the retainer in cash.

The men shook hands, and Dr. Williams departed to return to his home and medical practice two hours away in Richmond.

Bill Franklin had just irrevocably stepped into the case that would change his life.

Bill Franklin sat alone after Williams left. He ordered another drink, lit yet another Marlboro, and thought about the social milieu of Virginia Beach during the 1980's and about Chuck Robb, the man whose life he was about to expose.

Chapter Two

The Way We Were

"He was cool. He was no different from the rest of us."
A former party-goer to Bill Franklin

There had always been pockets of real affluence in Virginia Beach. For the most part, however, that affluence was connected to family names rich with history, social register connections, and status founded on contributions to the larger good. It was "old money." By the late 1970's, Virginia Beach was changing: the money was coming fast and it was coming easy. The children and grandchildren of generations of hard work and success found themselves with pockets full of cash. Long-held family farmlands were being sucked up by developers, sending the price of land in the burgeoning city skyrocketing.

And there was more money to be made too, lots of new money, in businesses that would thrive on the increase of disposable income. In a city where people once thought that a kosher hot dog meant the meat was accompanied by sauerkraut, the level of sophistication grew along with the ready cash and paper deals. Trendy restaurants were booming, and chic, up-scale boutiques catering to the wives and women of the men who were making the money blossomed in newly-born shopping areas, clustered wherever engineers could drive a new road and the real estate slicks could cadge another percentage. Real estate prices soared at Virginia Beach during those years, catapulted just as much by the excesses of the Reagan decade as they were by an ever-increasing population. Waterfront or waterfront proximity was and is an American obsession. But more so at Virginia Beach where the taints of Palm Beach, the Hamptons or Malibu had yet to make their claim.

Thousands of acres of farmland were bought up by developers. The buying and selling of property became so profitable that many people left other lucrative professions to take part in it, or, at the least, added real estate to their repertoire of business dealings.

It seemed as if the sand had turned to gold.

Many riding the crest of this shimmering wave were the beach boys of the late 60's, the kids who had grown up at and around the Beach. Many of them had gone to high school together; some left for college, and then rejoined one another when they returned. Some came from money; many did not. But the ones without financial status knew the ones who had it. And that, in Virginia Beach just as elsewhere, can often be everything. Or at least enough for a viable beginning.

They bought restaurants of their own; they went into businesses their fathers had worked hard to build. Some were professionals: doctors, lawyers, dentists. The money they made went into other business deals. It seemed, for a while, as if the money multiplied almost magically. They looked in their mirrors in the morning and were well pleased. In their reflection, they saw success as they had learned it from television. And, as the first television generation, they knew all the accoutrements of success.

They had fine cars; they had big boats. They had ornamental women, some of them the wives who had come through the years with them and some, the younger ones, who had gravitated toward the glitter the men spread around. Jaguars, Hatteras yachts and slim blonds dotted the landscape.

And they had cocaine. People who had money to invest saw coke as a hot commodity. People whose lives had been, if not exactly conservative, at least fairly straight up to that time, found themselves enthralled not only with the effect of the drug but with its extraordinary potential for increased wealth. It became, as one of them said, an integral part of the larger image and vision. As recently as the early 1980's, many physicians and other experts in the field of addiction believed that cocaine was essentially a relatively harmless, non-addictive recreational drug. Although its psychological effects were exceedingly enjoyable — the immediate rush, the clarity and seeming perfection of ideas, the heightened, almost electrifying sense of sexuality — physical addiction for occasional users was thought to be unlikely.

By the middle of the decade, however, the evidence showed otherwise. Occasional users who had become as addicted - physically and psychologically — as any heroin junkie began to turn up in treatment centers and emergency rooms all over the country. In one research study, rats that were given a choice between food, sex and cocaine repeatedly chose the cocaine. Until they died.

"The one bad thing about cocaine," said Dr. William Farley, an addictionologist, in a 1986 interview, "is that you don't get many chances with it before it's got you. And then you'll do anything to get it."

"The one good thing about cocaine," one joke goes, "is that you never have to worry about leftovers."

There were few leftovers in Virginia Beach. Cocaine became one of the most plentiful commodities around. As one party-goer said, cocaine also became the great equalizer. It blurred the class distinctions that in other years had been clear-cut demarcations between the haves and the have-nots. The drug brought together wealthy people, working people and street people who would not have come into contact with one another at any other time, at any other place, in any other way. Cocaine was also one of the most lucrative commodities to be found, and that was just as quickly discovered by the ambitious beach boys in Virginia Beach as anywhere else in America.

They brought cocaine back covered in softball skin, packed so tightly that the stitching showed on the white ball when it was unwrapped. They brought cocaine in on boats and they brought cocaine in on commercial passenger flights, tucked neatly under seats in innocuous-looking briefcases while former beach boys sat above it, drenched in sweat from fear that they'd be discovered. In the late 1970's the cocaine came with the other spoils of affluence. And from 1982 to 1987, during Chuck Robb's term as governor, it was a mainstay at parties and in the homes of some of the most successful men and women in Virginia Beach. The sellers had no trouble, no trouble at all, finding buyers in the wealthy young crowd at the heart of the social scene.

"We had all risen to a certain level," one of them said, raising his hand to shoulder height, "and we had it all. The only thing left to do was to go on to another level and have even more. More experiences. More fun.

"Cocaine," he said, as he raised his hand even higher, "was the next level."

Cocaine became the ever-present guest at private parties and public gatherings alike. During those years, it was a rare member of the in-crowd who didn't carry a vial of cocaine; some were equipped with "bullets" on the top so the user could snort while on the move. The drug was so plentiful that users were cavalier about where they used it and how they handled it. One former nightclub owner told of sweeping spilled cocaine off his club floor at night after closing.

"I'd have a whole handful," he recalled, "and I'd use it myself."

People came in with pockets full of coke and used it openly. Cocaine became the best means of entry into the very best crowd, the very hippest places. And the prettiest women.

Men whose appearance would not have turned a single head a year before — men whose looks and lifestyle and background should have prohibited them from being acknowledged by the more successful and attractive — suddenly arrived in long, sleek limousines, in the company of the kind of women who made other men gasp.

"You couldn't get laid if you didn't have coke," one man said, "but if you did. . .oh, if you did you could be as ugly as sin and get the most beautiful women. They'd screw anyone if they could get cocaine."

Unlike the professional prostitutes, whose primary form of barter was cash for sex, the coke whores craved the drug. And the coke whores, with no other entry to this Virginia Beach society except their bodies and their love of cocaine, became part of the show. They were young, in their late teens and early 20's. Some were the privileged daughters of affluent families; many were from middle class families with an eye on the fast lane. "They wanted to be part of us, the beautiful people," said one of the men. "They'd do anything — anything — to run with us. "We rode in limousines, we got naked, three couples would be screwing in the back, all at the same time," he added, grinning at the memory. "We had a hell of a good time."

Certain places, certain parties, certain people became the stuff of talk and growing legends. Croatan Beach was one of those places.

From the air, you can see its natural isolation from the main resort strip, cut off at the north by a thin ribbon of Rudee Inlet that leads into the Atlantic Ocean, and at the south by Lake Christine and the Naval Base, Dam Neck. To the west, Lake Wesley forms yet another moat-like natural barrier between Croatan and the traffic on General Booth Boulevard. Its very isolation and inaccessibility caused Croatan to be overlooked in the early years of Virginia Beach's emergence as a resort. For years, it was nearly forgotten by wealthy residents who favored instead the long-established North End as a refuge from the tourists who descended on the southern end of the beach, replete with its gaudy T-shirt vendors, souvenir shops and a teeming boardwalk.

But Croatan came to life in the late 1970's, budding with new construction of modern and ostentatious beach "cottages." The isolation and inaccessibility that had once been detriments became the predominant inducements to buy for those who could afford the property itself and then the multi-storied homes to fill the sandy lots. All the houses are different and all are spectacular, with prices well above half a million dollars. Enormous windows everywhere and balconies jutting out at staggered levels afford unobstructed views of the ocean.

An enclave of wealth, Croatan also grew into an architectural stewpot, symbolic of this oceanfront's rapidly growing money. It was as if someone had taken traditional beach cottages — with their weathered wood and summer porches — and amplified them in every conceivable way both inside and out: bigger rooms, more skylights, more and different wood, three fireplaces, a hot tub, and of course the requisite geranium pots and copper wind chimes punctuating the glossiness.

Naturally the new arrivals at Croatan fleshed out their television image of themselves with the obligatory BMW or Mercedes in the driveway.

A government reserve abuts Croatan. There, at Camp Pendleton, the Virginia National Guard base located just to the south of the resort strip, the state of Virginia maintains a modest cottage reserved for the sitting governor of the Commonwealth.

There are two ways to get to the governor's cottage. One is through the front gate, where a security guard logs the coming and going of all visitors. The other is through a private back gate, a gate to which the governor has a key. That gate leads to Croatan and is within walking distance of the homes there. When Charles Robb ascended to the Governor's mansion, the key to the back gate at Camp Pendleton was given to him. Through this gate Robb traveled between his two worlds of public propriety and private partying. Croatan was his. And the parties were underway.

All night parties, with all the cocaine you could possibly want, coke whores, paid prostitutes, and wild sex. The drug and its aura seemed to remove fear from the men and women involved. They talked openly among themselves, and to others, about who was there and where and when. And how.

They felt insulated against the outside world; they gave no thought to morality or illegality. They were rich, they were having fun, all the participants were willing and they were on top of the world.

There seemed to be no shame in Virginia Beach in 1982 — and in the five years to come — only hubris of the type that makes people believe they are invulnerable, invisible.

Cocaine overflowed out of Croatan. Many of the resort strip clubs were wide open: cocaine was used on the dance floor, in the service areas, behind the bars and in the bathrooms, which were also a favorite spot for sex. One man who was a part of all of it recalls being in a ladies' room, snorting coke with two women while one of them performed oral sex on him.

"The bouncer was at the door, hollering for us to come on out. When he finally broke in, he took one look and said, 'Ohhhh mannnnn. . . .'"

When the stories were told, names were repeated over and over, concentric circles moving in from the peripheral hangers-on to the ones in the inner circle.

Among the repeated names a big name kept coming up. His name came up as if this man were no different from the others, just another successful, wealthy, attractive guy snorting coke, another married man having sex with young women, another party person around the Beach for the good times.

His name came up because the others bragged about having him around. They bragged about what a good time they'd shown him, and they remarked on what a regular guy he was.

"A regular guy." Maybe. He seemed to act like the other men when it came to the drugs and the women. But he had a title and a position that set him apart from the rest of the crowd. When they swapped stories about him, the Beach people used his first name because they felt that he was one of them. "He was cool," said one man who was there. "He was no different from the rest of us."

They certainly never used his title because they didn't need to. And they didn't feel that they had to be protective of him because, in a way, they were protected by him, by his very presence in the midst of their illegal activities.

"I never felt so safe as when he was there," one man said. "I knew that as long as he was there, no dogs were coming in, and no cops."

Everyone knew who they meant. And what he was.

Beginning in 1982, the name that kept coming up, the name on all their lips, the name that ricocheted off the mirrored walls, bounced around the cabins of expensive yachts, across restaurant tables, and drifted out over the sand was the name of Virginia's Governor, Charles S. "Chuck" Robb.

Chapter Three

The Politician

*"There's no greater weight to bear than someone
else's dreams, and Robb's shoulders sometimes
slump a bit beneath the burden. But what's a guy
to do when he's the perfect presidential candidate?"*
Regardie's Magazine, October 1990

Charles Robb first stepped into Virginia Beach's
emerging picture of money, sex and drugs when he was
Lieutenant Governor of Virginia from 1977 to 1981.
Virginia Beach's appeal as a resort is the same for state
leaders as it is for tourists from Idaho, and so it was to the
Beach that Robb came, in his own words, "to let his hair
down. . .to be a normal human being." Born in Phoenix,
Arizona, on June 26, 1939, Charles Spittal Robb had a
difficult time being just "a normal person" once he began
his courtship of President Johnson's daughter, Lynda
Bird, in the summer of 1967. Sometime after his graduation from the University of Wisconsin, Robb had been
assigned to the White House Marine Corps detail as a
military social aide. One day, Robb was asked to sit in as
a fourth at bridge with Lynda Bird and her friends. Robb
soon replaced actor George Hamilton as Lynda Bird
Johnson's escort, a turn of events which reportedly was
much to Lyndon Johnson's relief.

The couple spent Labor Day weekend in 1967 at
Rehobeth Beach, Delaware, and were married on December 9, 1967, in the first wedding held at the White House
since 1914. They moved to a home in the wealthy suburb
of McLean, Virginia, where Massachusetts Senator Teddy
Kennedy and Virginia's Republican Senator John Warner
would be their neighbors.

Robb was adamant about wanting to serve in Vietnam, and so the young Marine left his wife behind. At the time, she was pregnant with the first of their three daughters, and she lived in the White House until he returned. In a 1989 interview, Lynda Robb recalled with a laugh that the one thing she had been sure of was that she did not want to marry a politician.

"I thought I was marrying a general," she said. According to published reports, Lynda's resolve to steer the remainder of her life away from the political arena was strengthened during Robb's tour in Vietnam as she lay awake in her White House bedroom listening to protesters outside taunting her father. She already had enough of the fishbowl life of politics. She didn't want it for herself and she didn't want it for her children.

It is difficult to determine now when Lynda Robb might have had the first inkling that the theme of her life as the daughter of a politician was going to continue to play out through her adulthood as a wife and mother, despite her determination to avoid it.

When Chuck Robb returned from Vietnam in 1970 decorated with the Bronze Star for bravery and the Vietnamese Cross of Gallantry, he still looked like the apolitical soldier she had dreamed of, but it is hard to imagine that she did not notice how much like Lyndon Johnson her husband was — confident, competent, ambitious. He graduated from the University of Virginia Law School in 1973, and went on to serve for a year as law clerk to Justice John D. Butzner of the Fourth U.S. Circuit Court of Appeals, after which he joined the Washington law firm of Williams, Connolly & Califano.

In the same 1989 interview with Walt Harrington of The Washington *Post*, Robb himself says of his emerging interest in politics that "It was a fairly gradual thing." Although Lynda pleaded against it — "I've been there and you haven't," she told him — by 1976 he made up his mind to run for lieutenant governor of Virginia.

The general she'd hoped for had turned into Daddy.

The state where Chuck Robb chose to stake his political fortunes has a rich past and Virginia Beach is an integral part of the state's historical tapestry.

From the first time white men set foot on its sandy shore four centuries ago and described it as one of the most beautiful beaches on earth, Virginia Beach and its adjacent land has lured settlers and visitors alike.

The boom that would eventually lead to a world-class resort began during the 1800's. By 1890, there were 14 cottages and several new hotels along the seven-mile beachfront. By the turn of the century, there was a jail, a town hall, a mayor and a policeman.

During the 1930's and 1940's, the clubs in Virginia Beach drew top-drawer entertainers to nightspots such as the Cabaret Beach Club, the Surf Club, the Terrace Club and the Peacock Ballroom at Seaside Park. Rudy Vallee, Tommy Dorsey, Fred Waring, Cab Calloway — they all passed through. Scott and Zelda Fitzgerald stayed at the stately Cavalier Hotel when they were in town.

Gambling also thrived. Virginia Beach had developed a reputation for being the East Coast answer to Las Vegas. All illegal, of course.

By the 1960's, 180,000 people lived there. Two decades later, the population had doubled so that by the spring of 1988, there were 364,300 citizens living in a city with a land mass of 258 square miles that sported 38 miles of shoreline.

Virginia Beach is only two hours away from the state capital at Richmond and within a one-hour air hop to Washington, D.C. Home to four large military installations and joined to the surrounding cities of Norfolk, Portsmouth, and Chesapeake, Virginia Beach is of the utmost strategic importance to national defense. Any governor or senator compromised by the use of illegal drugs represents a threat to the nation; it is difficult to imagine, however, any other state where that compromise through blackmail or bribery could place so much in jeopardy.

Virginia Beach is a fairly wealthy city, with median income around $34,000. It is, in some ways, a city for the young as well; the average age of its citizens is just 30. In many ways, its youth has given the oceanfront the image of California East. And it is a city whose focal point has hardly changed in 100 years. Despite a century of growth out from its initial roots, stretching its tentacles into farmlands, despite the malls and condos and cluster communities that seem to spring up overnight and tax the city's resources to their limits, despite the ever-growing population and the covering of concrete over much of the terrain, one singular thing is still the main attraction.

It is the same thing that made Sir Walter Raleigh's scouts' hearts beat fast 300 years ago, and it is the same thing that draws the people and the money and, especially, the people with the money.

It is the Beach.

And it was to that glorious beach that Chuck Robb came when he wanted to win an election, and afterwards, victorious.

The only election Robb has ever lost was in 1961, when he was defeated for the office of president of his graduating class at Wisconsin. It would be 16 years before he would run again, but, by the time he wanted to be lieutenant governor of Virginia, economic and political support systems were in place to assist him to victory. He had become, in the words of one interviewer, "a Democratic money magnet. . .linked to that magical [Johnson] name."

It was difficult for Robb to shake the "president's son-in-law" image, even if he had wanted to. During the race for lieutenant governor, for instance, hardly a press story appeared that didn't tie him to Johnson and the reference became part of almost every introduction on the campaign trail. When he visited a turkey hatchery in Harrisonburg during that spring, tour guide Taylor Grizzard introduced Robb to the workers by saying, "This is Chuck Robb, whose wife was President Johnson's daughter." If the press and public didn't let him forget it, neither did his wife. In his *Post* interview, Harrington reports an incident on the campaign trail toward the lieutenant governor's office when, after a disagreement over political tactics, Lynda told Chuck in front of on-lookers, "It's my money, after all." In 1977, when Robb garnered 54 percent of the vote and carried all of the state's ten congressional districts to become lieutenant governor, he was the only Democrat to persevere in a statewide Republican sweep of major offices. He rode his superior name recognition, strong financial backing and conservative support to a relatively easy victory. Robb left his law practice in order to devote all of his time and energies to being lieutenant governor, a $16,000-a-year position that had been, for his predecessors, a ceremonial, part-time job.

Within his first year as lieutenant governor, the press was already alluding to his next step.

The Washington Post called him the "only statewide figure acceptable to all philosophical factions of the [Democratic] party" and "its chief hope" for a Democratic governor. In the same article, Senate Majority Leader Adelard L. Brault acknowledged Robb as the titular head of the Democratic party. "The people of Virginia have gotten to know him and they like him," Brault said. "I think he's going to be our next governor." The Chuck Robb the people of Virginia had come to know was a man who was once described as "so straight you could use him to draw a line." Even his mother, Frances Howard Robb, said at one time, "Charles was born old and serious." He didn't drink coffee; he drank milk. The spit-shine, short-haired, tightly wrapped image of the former Marine en-dured.

In some ways, that reserved image worked against him. By the end of his second year as lieutenant governor, there were indications that the political tide might be turning against him. In a December 1979 story in *The Washington Post*, one prominent Democrat called Robb "a potential disaster." Another called him "remote" and said that his quietness and refusal to speak out on issues had left the people of Virginia not knowing what he stood for "or if he stands for anything."

This reticence was a life-long trait. Robb's father, James, once said of his son, "Charles plays things closer to the belt than anybody I've ever known."

Robb's rejoinder to the public's claim of remoteness was to say, "I make a deliberate attempt not to be too quotable. I find it difficult to give simplistic answers to complicated questions."

His political strength seemed to have been recovered by the following summer, although his image as a serious politician — as opposed to what one supporter called "glad handers" — remained and troubled some Virginia Democrats.

In August 1980, when the Democratic National Convention was held in New York City, his party connections were called "impeccable," and he moved easily among national and state party leaders, even while some delegates groused that he was not spending enough time on the convention floor, acting the part of a politician on the rise.

"He'll take a weekend trip to go to Danville to cut a ribbon, but you won't see him much among the delegation," one convention-goer complained.

Another delegate said, "I spend 30 percent of my total political life talking about Chuck Robb. His name comes up at every cocktail party, with every person, with every group, and I don't initiate it. Church groups, law partners, people in the state party — they all have a universally perceived question about him." The question, the delegate explained, was why Robb didn't act more like a politician and a man who covets higher office.

One delegate from Northern Virginia had an answer: "The guy has charted his course and you're going to see it through 1981." Robb made two speeches to the convention: one opposing a proposed freeze on development of nuclear weapons, the second a spirited pep talk for the party. Virginia conventioneers erected a makeshift "Robb for Governor" sign in the delegation.

Less than a year later, that makeshift placard proved prophetic. At their state convention in May 1981, the Democrats nominated Charles Robb as their candidate for governor. The ascendancy commenced.

Chapter Four

The Players

"Lucinda [Robb] says her mother with hard-earned and unerring political intuition had warned Chuck early on: 'I'm not sure I approve of that crowd.'"
The Washington Post, July 9, 1989

"The kindest thing you can say about Chuck Robb and his beach-partying days is that he has been surpassingly naive. Robb. . .regularly hobnobbed with people who trafficked in, consumed or condoned cocaine."
"The person who seems to have led the innocent lamb to the altar of perdition is Bruce Thompson."
The Roanoke Times & World News
September 1988

By the time Robb was preparing to run for governor, men like Bruce Thompson, Ed Ruffin, Ricky Haycox, Gene Schmidt, Marty Pallazio and Don Kern were in positions to personally donate, or help to raise, substantial amounts of money for the campaign. They became the strongest — and often the most visible — of his Virginia Beach supporters, and they were the men with whom he had already begun to socialize by the time he became governor in 1982.

Thompson was introduced to Robb while he was lieutenant governor. By the time Robb was governor, Thompson was his closest associate in Virginia Beach, a tie that would be often mentioned in later newspaper stories. Thompson bragged about his friendship with the governor and spared no expense in showing him off, and showing him a good time, when Robb was in town.

"Bruce wore Chuck Robb like a pretty new jacket," said one observer. "He just loved to show him off to anyone who would look. Bruce loved what being with Robb did for his image. And he tripped all over himself doing things for Chuck." Whatever Chuck wanted, Bruce got for him. Including prostitutes and cocaine.

By that time, too, Thompson and some of his business associates were also becoming known to Virginia state police authorities who were conducting surveillance during an undercover operation called "Operation Seagull."

Although their relationship had been open and common knowledge at Virginia Beach for several years, the first public linking of Robb to this group came in late August, 1983, in an Associated Press story carried by the Norfolk-based *The Virginian-Pilot and The Ledger-Star*. The headline on the first story said, "Robb Went Fishing on Criminal's Boat."

The story reported that Robb had gone on a fishing trip aboard Ricky Haycox's boat, "Morning Star." Frederick "Ricky" Haycox III had inherited a bankrupt asphalt and concrete business from his father and turned it into a success. Acquaintances give Haycox credit for being a hard worker and an astute businessman, while assessing him as one of the wealthiest men in Virginia Beach.

In 1981, Haycox was convicted on federal charges of rigging bids on highway projects in the Hampton Roads area. As president of the Asphalt Roads & Materials Co., Inc., Haycox served a 60-day prison term and was fined $15,000. His company was fined $150,000. But it could have been worse if he hadn't testified for the prosecution against other defendants.

Haycox's boat, "Morning Star," a 54-foot Hatteras sport fisher valued between $600,000 and $800,000, was a favorite floating party spot.

George Stoddart, a spokesman for Robb, said that the governor did not know that Haycox owned the boat, nor did he know that Haycox had pleaded guilty two years earlier to federal bid-rigging charges.

The fishing trip was arranged for Robb by Bruce Thompson, and the men were joined by Ed Ruffin. Haycox was at the helm of the boat for the day and Stoddart said that Robb thought Haycox was just the fishing boat captain and that Ruffin was the owner. Thompson had attended numerous parties and social events with both Robb and Haycox by that time. Thompson is well known for his astuteness and good memory; he is also such a stickler for detail that he often tape records office conversations in a somewhat Nixonian fashion. When members of the press questioned Thompson, he publicly explained his gaff of arranging a trip for the governor on a boat belonging to, and driven by, a convicted felon by saying, "Hell, I never even thought about who owned the boat."

It was the first of many public statements about Chuck Robb's social life that would clink like cheap tin.

Bruce L. Thompson was a 1970 graduate of First Colonial High School who attended Virginia Polytechnical Institute for two years. He began his business career in ski equipment rentals and as a promoter of skiing trips. He also worked as an ID checker at the door of The Raven, a resort strip restaurant owned by twin brothers, Ricky and Bobby Dunnington, with whom he had been friends for years. It was through the ski trips, newly popular at the Beach, that Thompson expanded his realm of acquaintances to doctors, attorneys, and businessmen.

People who know him say that Bruce Thompson is the quintessential showman. On a "Cruise to Nowhere" junket, the entertainers appeared in a conga line wearing Carmen Miranda costumes, including headpieces replete with artificial fruit. According to another shipboard guest, Thompson grabbed real fruit from a serving tray and began to put it on his head, in his shirt pocket, and anywhere he could make it stick out of his clothes, before joining the paid entertainers. The crowd loved it.

Thompson is also known as a good salesman, the eternal public optimist with a knack for turning a potential disaster into an adventure that garners grins.

The weather had turned warm for skiing on the day before one of the trips for which he was to be the coordinator. At the party held at Pascal's, a favorite Beach spot, the night before the busload of people were scheduled to leave, there was much grumbling about the weather. According to one novice skier who was there, Thompson got up before the hostile crowd and convinced them that they were about to have a hell of a good time.

"When he was finished," the man said, "they were eating out of his hand and they couldn't wait to get on that bus."

On another occasion, a Super Bowl junket Thompson had arranged threatened to go bad when there were problems with the chartered plane picking up the passengers on time. Grumbling had begun and tempers were fraying by the time the group finally boarded.

"I have no idea how he did it," one of those who had been unhappy said, "but when we landed, there was Bruce as we got off the plane, handing out T-shirts that read, 'We lost the plane but we won the game!' The last thing anybody remembers from that trip is that they went home laughing."

"This guy," said a buddy of Thompson's, "can be a scream." People who have worked closely with and for him say he can be a scream in other ways too. There is a darker side to Bruce Thompson, they say, one with a vicious temper, and abrasive personality, a propensity for drinking to oblivion and an eye that sees people entirely in terms of their social class.

"Mystique" and "charisma" are words that come up when people talk about Bruce Thompson. He is smart, they say, even brilliant, in his ability to associate with people who can be of assistance to him and to ingratiate himself with them.

"He seems like a great guy when you're with him," one former business partner said, "but make no mistakes. Bruce's first concern is Bruce."

The people who were at the parties talked openly about how Thompson paid the prostitutes who had become a regular part of the party scene and he made sure the cocaine was on hand.

In 1982, Bruce Thompson was renting a house at Croatan where many of the most-talked-about parties took place.

Eugene "Gino" Schmidt rented the Croatan house with Bruce Thompson. Schmidt, then 40, started with a single sub/sandwich shop called Zero's in the early 1970's and expanded the operation into an extremely successful chain throughout the Hampton Roads area. In addition, he went into real estate investment when the boom began. Tall and handsome, Schmidt was described by a woman who knew him as "a womanizer, a sucker for a pretty face but the kind of guy who always had to be in charge."

When people talk about Gene Schmidt and his cousin Marty Pallazio, they say their names almost as one: "Gene-and-Marty." In addition to being related, the two men were roommates and business associates.

Donald Kern, who was 43 in 1982, was another beach boy who had done well. A graduate of the prestigious prep school, Norfolk Academy, and the Virginia Military Institute, and first in his class in dental school, Kern was the one the newspapers would eventually refer to as the "golden boy," to whom wealth and success had always seemed to come easily. Kern also went into real estate when it seemed at least as lucrative as working on teeth. By his own admission, his income during the mid-1980's was around $800,000 to $900,000 a year and he "wouldn't consider touching a [real estate] deal that was less than $10 million." Kern built a $1.4 million house at Croatan a few doors down from Thompson and Schmidt, complete with a reflecting pool in the foyer and a spiral staircase that wrapped around the built-in waterfall cascading into a garden. There was also a hot tub on the roof.

Gregarious, aggressive and flashy, Kern sported tinted aviator eyeglasses and drove a gold-painted Mercedes. Curiously, however, as good as it might have looked on his tanned arm, the Rolex he wore was a copy.

People who had known Kern for many years — before, during and after his cocaine use — said that he is brilliant, with an IQ in the genius range. Professional associates said he was an excellent dentist.

That's where the compliments end. An uncontrollable temper and an apparent inability to tell the truth combine with a smooth and charming manner to present a picture that people around him call classic Jekyll and Hyde.

Then there were Richard and Robert Dunnington, twin brothers who were in their late 30's, and friends of Bruce Thompson's. Ricky and Bobby owned The Raven, a casual restaurant and descendant of the 1970's fern bars, where Bruce Thompson had worked in 1974. One of the fruits of the Dunnington's success from that business was the "Sea Raven," a 39-foot dark blue O'Day sailboat with Kelly green striping.

John Bennis, who was 32 in 1982, a clothing wholesaler, also lived at Croatan with his wife Gina. They were hosts for, and guests at, many of the parties. One particular birthday party given for Bennis by his wife was held on the top floors of the Ocean Ranch hotel. Several hundred people packed the rooms that were open for their pleasure, while others danced beside the rooftop pool. That particular party would become memorable because of one special guest: Chuck Robb.

Wilfred "Billy" O'Dell, among the youngest men in the crowd at age 24, was a former stockbroker and restaurateur who came to be known as one of the most reliable cocaine dealers in town. With a Bachelor's degree from Virginia Wesleyan College and a solid middle-class background, O'Dell's life exemplified the jagged turn so many lives took during those years, wrecked by cocaine.

Chapter Five

The Politician's Protagonist

> *"I cuss like hell, drink a little whiskey. I'll go anywhere and talk to anyone from college professors to whores, and I'm at home just about wherever I go."*
>
> Bill Franklin
> The Danville Register, 1988

They said Billy Austin Franklin was the best private investigator in the state and had been, ever since he came to Virginia Beach in 1963. And a lawyer too. It was what his mother had always wanted. So he'd done it and he'd done it the hard way: read the law, four hours a day, five days a week and a half-day on Saturday, and spent two summers auditing courses at the College of William and Mary in Williamsburg, Virginia. It took him three and a half years, and the bar exam whipped him twice until finally, in 1983, at the unlikely age of 48, he was admitted to the bar.

Good, thorough, tough. That's what he was.

He had turned 53 on March 20, 1988, and he had been married to the same woman, Marquitta "Keetie" Klein Franklin, for 28 years. He was the namesake founder of Franklin Security Systems, Inc., a private investigative company housed in a modest brick building in a working man's section of Norfolk, Virginia, 15 miles and a huge lifestyle leap from the Virginia Beach waterfront home where he lived on a bluff overlooking a serene bay.

No one would call him pretty. His voice rumbles up from deep in his belly and his eyes hold fast on friend and foe alike. When he grins, his face looks like Christmas morning. When he glowers, he seems to look back inside himself at a dark place no one else would want to go. His reputation precedes him everywhere.

The man Bill Franklin had become in middle age had evolved naturally from the boy who smiles endearingly from old family photo albums. Clean cut, scrub-faced, and somehow always right smack in the middle of every group photo. His drive not only to excel but to win seems to have been there from his earliest days. In 1947 when the Cub Scouts from the Chula Vista Pack 393 gathered for their annual honors party, the local newspaper arrived for a photo opportunity and the story that would become Bill Franklin's first publicity. After a few paragraphs on the party, there is this:

"Especially honored at the party was Billy Franklin, sixth grade student, who received all the honors it is possible for a Cub Scout to receive, including the Lion badge, gold and silver arrows, Webelos and graduation. This is the first time [in the pack] any Cub was eligible for all these honors. . .Billy Franklin is not quite 12 years old."

After that, the clippings begin to build like some inexorable wave. There are sports stories when he played linebacker and fullback in football and third base in baseball in high school and then football in college; there are notices praising his acting in college comedies and dramas.

Bill Franklin has never been shy. The performer seems to have been there from the beginning as well. In grade school he played the clarinet. In junior high and high school, he switched to the saxophone. In high school, he had a choice: to be in the marching band or to be on the football team. He picked football. He is, in many ways, a "man's man." The intelligence, agility, strength and power necessary to succeed in football are exactly the qualities he prizes so highly in himself and others, and to which he seems to have gravitated from the beginning of his life.

It is no surprise, then, that the late Vince Lombardi, coach of the champion Green Bay Packers, is one of his heros.

A copy of Lombardi's speech, "What It Takes To Be Number One," hangs on Bill Franklin's office wall. The words are cast into a bronze plaque beneath a likeness of

Lombardi, and the plaque hangs amidst dozens of certificates, awards and similar plaques that Franklin has received over the years.

"You've got to pay the price. Winning is not a sometime thing. It's an all the time thing. You don't win once in a while, you don't do things right once in a while. You do them right all the time."

Bill Franklin holds that attitude toward everything about himself: his education, his sports, his job, his family, his life. He does not believe there's much value in second place. He has never backed down. Not from anything. The stories are legion, legend. The leader of the motorcycle gang whose cronies had broken the collarbone of one of his employees would tell you how Franklin came to the parking lot the next night and told them: "Move your fuckin' bikes." Street tough, brazen, no one moved anything. Franklin ran his van over the leader's motorcycle. Forward first. Then in reverse. He lumbered from the van, a .357 Colt leering from his waistband and a sawed-off shotgun in his hand. Everyone moved.

Everyone remembered.

"That big crazy white motherfucker," they said.

The punk who stole the beer remembered too. There was a party at the man's house — the $600,000 house on the water, the house that damned hard work had built — and the kid came around, thinking no one would notice him carting off a keg of beer. Bill Franklin noticed. He held the kid up against the wall by the front of his shirt, raising him up to eye level with those big, meaty hands with a one-karat diamond Masonic ring on one hand and a 3/4-inch gold Austrian ducat on the other. He barked into the kid's face, his own face turning beet red and sweat pouring off his bald pate.

"If you don't get the hell out of here right now I am going to bite off your head and shit down your neck!"

So the legend grew, and although the toughness was important, it was more important that people knew he was fair. Straightforward. Patient in his investigations. And kind, kind almost to a fault, to the people he liked.

"A teddy bear," his close friends said.

"But don't screw with him," they added.

By that spring of 1988, Bill and Keetie Franklin enjoyed a good life. Twelve years earlier, they had taken their first vacation in 14 years, a well-deserved respite in the Bahamas and the Florida Keys. It was off Key Largo that Bill tied into his first sailfish and became obsessed with the battle between man and big fish.

A man who goes after big fish needs a big boat and over the years Bill Franklin's had grown bigger. Later in 1976, when Bill and Keetie bought an acre of property on a bluff overlooking Broad Bay, the first thing they did was to build a pier. Two years later, in December 1978, they moved into the sprawling home they had built there.

At the end of their 200-foot pier, "Rum Runner," a 25-foot fishing boat, waited. They also owned a condominium at the oceanfront, and a 40-foot sport-fishing boat. "Top Hook" was primarily for charter trips, but they used it too. Bill and Keetie were looking forward to another summer of fishing for flounder, spot and croaker in the Chesapeake Bay, and marlin and tuna off the coast of Virginia and North Carolina.

Their daughter, Donna, had grown up smart and beautiful. In the spring of 1988 she was preparing to graduate from college.

In the morning you could find Bill Franklin working out at Wareing's Gym, the premier sweat shop at the Virginia Beach oceanfront. In the company of some of the best known names at the Beach, the wanna-be's and the serious muscle builders, Franklin fought back against the cigarettes and whiskey, both of which he consumed with unstoppable passion, and age, which was inexorable. He was in fine shape.

Everybody knew him, if not to speak to him directly at least to murmur an acknowledgement of his presence.

Bill and Keetie Franklin had the world by the tail.

But now, with the Robb case, Bill Franklin also had a tiger by the tail.

Chapter Six

Operation Seagull

"The rationale behind it [Operation Seagull] is something only the state police could answer. They're the ones who designed it, who ran it."
Commonwealth's Attorney Paul Sciortino
The Virginian-Pilot and The Ledger-Star
April 7, 1985

The years between the first newspaper story in 1983 that placed Robb on Ricky Haycox's boat and the beginning of Bill Franklin's investigation into Chuck Robb's cocaine use in May 1988 were busy ones for law enforcement officials, newspaper reporters and the group of Robb's Virginia Beach friends and associates.

The first published reports about Robb on Haycox's boat attracted the attention of local newspaper reporters and had them asking the question among themselves: what was Robb doing in the company of Haycox?

The reporters began to ask around, to listen. What they heard on the streets during 1984 and 1985 seemed to place Robb in the midst of the parties at Croatan, hotels and aboard yachts. Rose Ellen O'Connor came to work at *The Virginian-Pilot and The Ledger-Star*'s Virginia Beach office to cover Virginia Beach schools in 1984 after seven years as an investigative reporter for television stations in Washington, D.C. and Norfolk. She was assigned to the Robb story.

John Sherwood was another reporter who began to look into Robb's activities. Sherwood also worked out of the Virginia Beach office of *The Virginian-Pilot and The Ledger-Star*; the Virginia Beach courts were his beat.

Late in 1984, a tip came in to the newspaper's editors. Rose Ellen O'Connor was teamed with Sherwood to investigate further the rumors about Robb. Sherwood's early discussions with some of his law enforcement sources appeared to give credence to the stories.

Before the two reporters could fully explore Robb's activities, however, each was drawn to focus on other stories that seemed more important and more urgent. While Rose Ellen O'Connor joined other reporters to uncover Landbank, a multi-billion dollar second mortgage scandal, Sherwood's interest was directed to two cardboard cartons filled with documents pertaining to an undercover operation that had been delivered to Virginia Beach Commonwealth's Attorney, Paul Sciortino for prosecution of suspected gamblers.

Sherwood became suspicious of the amount of money spent on the undercover operation, which began in 1979. Code-named "Operation Seagull," it was a joint criminal investigation which the Virginia State Police Bureau of Criminal Investigation entered into at the request of the Virginia Beach Police Department as a result of what the local department believed to be an influx of known and suspected organized crime figures into the Virginia Beach area.

As part of that investigation, in November 1980, the Virginia Bureau of Criminal Investigation agents had followed a group of Virginia Beach businessmen to New York City for the wedding of the daughter of Anthony "Tony G" Gargulio.

Gargulio had a home and businesses in Virginia Beach and also maintained a home in Staten Island, New York. According to state police investigative documents, Gargulio is a reputed underworld figure said to be an "associate" of the Gambino crime family in New York.

What particularly caught the investigators' eyes, however, was that one of Gargulio's Virginia Beach business partners was Bruce Thompson, Charles Robb's connection to the Virginia Beach business and social community.

Bruce Thompson is shown in ten of the nearly 300 surveillance photographs of the Gargulio wedding processed by investigators in order to identify known members of crime families in attendance. Edward Garcia, a prominent, powerful Virginia Beach businessman and developer, and a well-known, flamboyant Norfolk attorney, were also photographed at the wedding.

Sherwood's first story on Operation Seagull was published on Easter Sunday in April 1985. It detailed the hundreds of thousands of dollars that the Virginia state police had spent on the undercover operation.

His coverage focused on the end result of the investigation, during which time special agent Louis Slade impersonated a high-rolling, wheeler-dealer in order to infiltrate illegal gambling operations. During the three years that Slade led people to believe he was "Larry Watson," he lost at least $150,000 of the taxpayers' money at gambling tables; thousands more were spent on maintaining "Watson's" luxurious lifestyle, which included a waterfront condominium, expensive meals and wine at Oceanfront restaurants, and travel.

Two years after the investigation was abruptly suspended by state police, some of the Operation Seagull files were brought to Commonwealth's Attorney Paul Sciortino for prosecution of gamblers caught in the undercover net.

What Sherwood and others found suspicious was that the expensive and lengthy investigation netted indictments of only eleven people, ten of whom pleaded guilty to reduced charges and paid a paltry total of $8,000 in fines, which ranged individually from $250 to $3,000. Charges were dropped against the eleventh man. None went to jail.

After discussions with his editors, Sherwood intended to follow the Operation Seagull story, investigating, in particular, the conflicting rumors about why the operation was shut down and a law enforcement tip that there had been a cover-up in the highest levels of state government.

It was also agreed that Sherwood would publish follow-up stories about the state House investigation that his original story had sparked, and a story about the Gargulio wedding as part of his Operation Seagull coverage.

Sherwood followed up on the state legislators' review; although dismayed, he was not surprised when the state officials publicly reported no irregularities with the state police investigation.

However, before Sherwood could publish the story of the New York wedding and the list of local guests, he found himself blocked by his editors.

He was dumbfounded. He couldn't comprehend why the editors would prevent publication of crucial investigative materials demonstrating ties between public officials and the mob. He was even more distressed that he was obstructed from exploring the allegations of a cover-up.

Despite repeated inquiries during the ensuing weeks and months, Sherwood was denied an adequate answer as to why the work was halted. Unable to resolve his disagreements with certain editors, including one who had familial ties to a target of the state police investigation, Sherwood agreed to leave the newspaper.

Before he left, however, in December 1985, he delivered his investigative files, including Operation Seagull secret documents, to a concerned editor who, with Sherwood, hoped that someday the full story would be reported.

A year later, another piece of the Operation Seagull story was reported, delving further into the same allegations that Sherwood had been thwarted from exploring. In December 1986, a Washington, D.C. area newspaper published facts about Virginia state police investigating mob influence in Virginia Beach. The local *Virginian-Pilot* and *Ledger-Star* followed up with a story of their own a week later. It was partly based on Sherwood's files which had been passed along to reporter Rose Ellen O'Connor. The final, edited story that appeared under the somewhat derisive headline WARNINGS OF ORGANIZED CRIME DRAW SKEPTICISM seemed to thumb its nose at the details in confidential law enforcement documents which had been turned over to the Virginia State Crime Commission. The investigative reports alleged that "traditional organized crime groups have been active in Virginia for the past 20 years. Members and associates of the New York-based Gambino crime family have conducted large illegal sports gambling operations in the Tidewater, Virginia area." Only one paragraph in the lengthy newspaper story dealt with the November 1980 Gargulio wedding. Although the newspaper reported that ". . .as part of the Seagull investigation, police followed Garcia and several other prominent Virginia Beach residents to the New York wedding. . .", neither Bruce Thompson nor any of the other guests was identified. Robb's social ties to Bruce Thompson and the Virginia Beach "fast lane" crowd had apparently gone unnoticed. Or unreported for some reason. For the second time in a year, *The Virginian-Pilot* and *The Ledger-Star* apparently had chosen to withhold critical information from its reading public.

Chapter Seven

The First Falls

"Former Gov. Charles S. Robb, who broke into Virginia politics in the 1970's by reaching out to the state's old guard, built a much different network of friends and acquaintances in this resort city during the early 1980's."

The Virginian-Pilot and Ledger-Star,
August 28, 1988

Virginia Beach has always retained a deceptive veneer of propriety for the millions of tourists who have flocked to its sandy beaches. Although it was fast becoming the glittering crown jewel and generator of revenue in a state that did not allow liquor by the drink until the early 1970's, Virginia Beach's apparent lack of sophistication hid an underbelly of illegal activities — most notably gambling — that came to be a thriving enterprise in the first half of the century. By the 1950's, the outraged citizens who were leading lives in more acceptable, legal pursuits stood behind the renegade owner and editor of a local weekly newspaper, The Virginia Beach Sun, trying to rid the city of the illegal profiteers and the political network that looked the other way.

So this is a city with a history of deception. The reality of Virginia Beach shimmers like sunlight on its waters. Beneath the surface, however, another culture prevails.

During the late 1970's, twenty years after the gambling was forced underground, the first in a series of federal grand juries was impaneled to hear testimony about drug use and trafficking in Virginia Beach. As the grand juries continued through the 80's, no quarter of Virginia Beach society was spared. Prominent names, prominent families, attorneys, businessmen, politicians: the tentacles of the probe touched them all.

By 1985, the third year of Robb's term as governor, yet another wave of witnesses was being called to appear before a federal grand jury to testify about cocaine use at Virginia Beach.

In the spring of 1987, almost exactly a year before Bill Franklin was hired by Dr. Williams, the latest lid blew off. The rumors that had circulated for so long became the stuff of public comment and front page headlines.

The Drug Enforcement Agency arrested dentist-turned-realtor Don Kern and restaurateur Billy O'Dell in their Oceanfront homes. Kern had been indicted by the federal grand jury and O'Dell was picked up on a criminal complaint. DEA agents said that they had moved on O'Dell before an indictment was returned because they had information that he was liquidating assets and apparently preparing to flee the area.

Both men were charged with using their homes and cars to facilitate the distribution of cocaine and, under the new "kingpin" law, faced the possibility of having their property confiscated.

As part of his plea bargain agreement with the U.S. Attorney's office through which he was allowed to plead guilty to one count of drug trafficking, Kern agreed to enter drug rehabilitation therapy and to testify about drug trafficking in Virginia Beach.

The word ripped through the community that testimony in the grand jury placed Chuck Robb at parties where cocaine was used and implicated him in cocaine use, although no allegations were made that he had trafficked in the drug.

In spite of the fact that grand jury testimony is privileged, scores of people from the Virginia Beach party scene were called to appear and, as one observer said, "there are only so many lawyers in this town and word gets out into the system." In early May 1987, the Richmond *Times-Dispatch* printed an article quoting a federal source as saying that Kern and other unidentified witnesses involved Robb in their grand jury testimony concerning cocaine use.

In a follow-up story by *The Virginian-Pilot* on May 4, Robb said that he could not remember meeting Kern, although federal authorities confiscated a photograph of the two men together when they searched Kern's Croatan home. Robb also said he had never been aware of being at a social event where anyone was using or possessing illegal drugs.

The photograph showing Robb and Kern together was discounted by Robb. He said, "Any politician poses for pictures hundreds of times. . . . There must be tens of thousands of photographs of me with other people."

In that same story, Kern insisted that he had only a passing acquaintance with Robb and knew nothing that would link Robb to drugs. Privately, however, he would say something else altogether.

Friends and acquaintances remember Kern's relationship with Robb differently, saying that Kern bragged about having used cocaine with Robb at parties, and that the two men often played golf together. Like many of the others who were sucked into the vortex of the drug probe, Kern remained publicly protective of Robb while privately enhancing his own image and position through their friendship.

In a follow-up story on May 17 in *The Washington Post*, Robb's friend, Hampton attorney Stephen Smith, jocularly said to *Post* reporter Donald Baker, "I guess you could say Chuck is a Coke addict. He's about cleaned me out of Coca-Cola." Robb was a frequent guest at Smith's Princess Anne Hills home.

Meanwhile, the Landbank second mortgage scandal was beginning to wind down. When the Richmond newspaper broke the story about Robb's connection to cocaine, reporter Rose Ellen O'Connor turned her attention once again to Robb's activities at Virginia Beach.

Chapter Eight

Power Plays

"They found me guilty and sentenced me, in absentia."

Lt. Gary Van Auken,
Virginia Beach Police officer

Although several years had elapsed since the height of cocaine use at Virginia Beach, the repercussions continued into 1988 when Bill Franklin first began to closely examine the events. The grand jury; the arrest, conviction and sentencing of Donald Kern and Billy O'Dell; and the drug-related arrest and subsequent jail house suicide of Ray Parsons, an electrical contractor who had acted as a major drug supplier for the Beach's in-crowd, combined with the scrutiny of reporter Rose Ellen O'Connor to create an electric atmosphere as Bill Franklin stepped into the scene in May 1988.

Ironically, Bill Franklin already knew most of the people whose names had come up during the investigations. As Franklin Security Systems had grown over the years, so had its client list. And the very things that Franklin was so good at — polygraphing dishonest employees, internal investigations and domestic surveillance — were exactly the services that these businessmen had needed over the years.

At the request of business owners, Franklin's staff had polygraphed employees who, first, admitted stealing goods to finance drug buys. Then they would admit using drugs at work. And then, when asked with whom they had used drugs, on more than one occasion an employee would admit that he'd been snorting cocaine with the boss.

Diane Heaney, who single-handedly managed the domestic case load for Franklin, remembered well the various men who strolled into the office, dropped thousands of dollars in cash on the desk, and requested that a wife or mistress be kept under surveillance while they traveled to South America "on business." She remembered, too, the comedy that ensued on one occasion when she was following a man and woman in a car and then realized that she was being followed as well. The passengers in the third car turned out to be DEA agents who were also watching the couple.

It was especially through wives who wanted their husbands watched that Heaney and Franklin began to become aware of how prevalent and pervasive cocaine use had become. More often than not, in describing a husband's habits or suggesting behavior to watch for, a wife would mention, "He's doing coke. So he's real paranoid."

The paranoia of cocaine users is legendary and it made the job of Heaney and her investigators more difficult as well as comedic.

"You've got to keep a real close eye on these guys," Heaney says. "They'll crouch around in the bushes right in front of their own homes, afraid someone's gonna get them. They're funny to watch, but it's pretty pitiful too."

The very people who had hired Bill Franklin to do their investigative work because they prized his tenacity and thoroughness were now his quarry. Stalked instead of stalker. And the worst part was that they knew from personal experience how good he was.

When Franklin began his interviews, he found many of the Beach habitues not only willing but anxious to talk about the former governor's presence and involvement in the party scene between 1982 and 1986, when he left office.

A sense of ill-will had filtered through the once-invulnerable crowd. Rumors flew concerning who said what to the grand jury. A number of people, including Bruce Thompson and Bobby and Ricky Dunnington, were granted immunity from prosecution for their testimony. John Bennis was granted immunity as well, and testified that cocaine use was common among his friends. Gene Schmidt was arrested on cocaine distribution charges at his Key West, Florida home as a result of the drug investigation but prosecutors dropped the charges when a key witness failed to corroborate allegations against him.

Alex Hargroves pleaded guilty and served 90 days in prison for failing to tell authorities that Ray Parsons had arranged drug deals from Old Dominion Engineering Inc., Hargroves' firm. Hargroves also testified in court in the fall of 1987 that he had been an addict for many years and had purchased cocaine from Parsons.

The mood in the community was a mix of emotions by the spring of 1988. Although some doors were slammed in his face. Bruce Thompson, for instance, refused to talk to him — Bill Franklin was surprised at how many people were not only willing but anxious to talk to him.

And how many people knew about Robb's involvement.

The real mystery around so much of what happened in Virginia Beach during Robb's term as governor from 1982 until 1986 is how a major political figure could have believed that he could move amidst the general public, use illegal substances, and never be caught. The secretive comradery of drugs, especially cocaine, gives a false illusion of invulnerability and, perhaps, invisibility. Perhaps he thought no one would notice.

More than likely, he thought no one would ever tell. Or worse, that he was totally invulnerable.

Within the first month of his investigation, Bill Franklin conducted over 40 interviews. His original belief that Robb could not possibly be connected to cocaine was destroyed as he listened to story after story about the parties where drugs were used openly in Robb's presence. Equally troubling were the stories involving Robb and women. Although Franklin had been adamant that he wasn't interested in investigating Robb's infidelities, he quickly realized that they were so obvious as to be unavoidable.

Bill Franklin was about to find out just how intertwined sex, money and power were within the tightly-knit group of Robb's friends.

Gary Van Auken was among the people Bill Franklin talked to during the first month of his investigation. The two men had known each other since Van Auken had first joined the police department. Franklin wanted Van Auken to explain a story Franklin had heard that involved Van Auken, Haycox and Thompson.

In that summer of 1988, Gary Van Auken was 41 years old and he had been a Virginia Beach police officer for almost 20 years. His brother, Paul, was convicted of interstate transportation and sale of illegal drugs; he was sentenced to federal prison in 1988.

Gary Van Auken is another who grew up with all the local guys at the Beach. He became friends with Ed Ruffin, Bruce Thompson, and Ricky Haycox. At one time he helped Thompson run ski trips. On two occasions, he skied at Aspen, Colorado, with Ruffin and Chuck Robb.

The governor, he said, was pleasant company and a good skier.

Van Auken told Franklin that in March 1987, Ricky Haycox invited him on a trip to the Bahamas. The men flew from Norfolk International Airport to Florida, where they picked up the "Morning Star" — the same boat on which the newspaper reported Chuck Robb had gone fishing — and sailed to the islands. In the midst of a costly divorce and raising his two children on his own, it was the kind of trip Van Auken could not have afforded on his own. Haycox picked up the tab for everything, an act of generosity not unusual in this circle of long-time friends. Aboard the boat, Van Auken, Haycox, boat captain Wendall "Wendy" Waggener and a mate set about to have a fine time. Fishing, scuba diving, sunning themselves while the folks back home battled chilled March winds. In the evenings, the four men sat on the deck, watching the sky and the stars. And, as groups of men tend to do, they got to talking about women.

And then they got to talking about Chuck Robb.

"The guy never ceases to amaze me," Haycox said to Van Auken. "He's got brass balls when it comes to women."

And then Waggener piped up with a story of his own. On one occasion, he said, when Robb was aboard the boat they were headed toward open water when Waggener looked out over the bow. There, before him, lay the governor, stark naked, surrounded by three nude women. As Waggener watched, stunned, the four rolled around together, engaged in sex play. Van Auken thought that if even part of this story were true, it was incomprehensible that the governor would compromise himself so openly.

When he spoke with Bill Franklin, Van Auken recalled that none of the men in the group seemed the least bit uncomfortable about telling these stories. There was no sense of secrecy, no pledge of confidentiality required. It was just, Van Auken said, "four guys sittin' around talkin' about pussy."

Several months later, in the spring of 1987, Gary Van Auken was in dire financial straits because of his divorce. He expressed his concern to his friend Ricky Haycox, who offered to help by arranging a loan at a low interest rate. Van Auken accepted his friend's generosity.

Haycox made a telephone call and then told Van Auken that a $15,000 loan had been arranged for him. All he had to do was to go see Harry Hampson, a vice-president at Crestar Bank, and sign the note.

Gary Van Auken never saw a loan application or a loan officer. Hampson welcomed him in his office and presented an already-prepared demand note, with interest only payable for a year. Van Auken explained to Hampson, as he had to Haycox, that in all probability he could not pay the note off in a year. Hampson reassured him, saying "Don't worry about it. Ricky says you're good for it and that's good enough for me." Van Auken was told that the loan would be renewed as long as he needed it; all he had to do was to make the interest payments on time each month.

With the loan, Van Auken was able to get on his feet financially and start turning his life around.

The year passed. It was not a good year for the group that included Haycox: scrutiny by the federal grand jury made everyone nervous and they began to carp among themselves. Paranoia began to set in. The stories about Chuck Robb were proliferating and becoming increasingly public.

By the spring of 1988, tempers were flaring around the Oceanfront. Van Auken, expecting the paperwork for the renewal of his note, received, instead, a call for full payment from Crestar Bank.

"I had to read the letter three times," he said. "I couldn't believe it."

He called his friend Ricky Haycox.

Haycox, who had once been so warm, friendly and helpful, was now cold, distant and abrupt.

"Hey," he told Van Auken, "that's how it goes sometimes with banks. I suggest you pay them."

Van Auken was stunned. Although he was re-establishing himself financially, he was a long way from being able to come up with $15,000 on the spot.

He wrote a letter to Harry Hampson, first saying how much he appreciated the loan, then pointing out that his interest payments had always been on time. Then he explained that it would be a hardship to pay off the entire note at that time, and offered to make a partial payment of several thousand dollars and switch the debt to a conventional loan.

It was a reasonable offer from a reasonable man.

The letter Van Auken received by return mail was curt, only two or three lines. It said, simply, that the terms he offered were unacceptable and that the bank would expect full payment on the date it was due.

Van Auken panicked. Faced with total financial ruin, he put his home on the market and, luck was with him, he sold it almost immediately. He borrowed $5,000 from his credit union, got $10,000 from the closing of the house on a Friday afternoon and was at the doorstep of Crestar Bank on Monday morning to pay his loan in full.

It seemed, he recalled, as if he had just had real bad luck with this bank.

A month later, Gary Van Auken realized he had been the victim of something darker than just bad luck.

A friend called Van Auken with a question. Did he, the friend wondered, have a note with Crestar that had just been pulled?

To the best of Van Auken's knowledge, only he, Haycox and Hampson had known about the loan, so Van Auken was surprised at the question.

When he answered affirmatively, the friend explained that Bruce Thompson accused Van Auken of being the source of rumors about Chuck Robb that had been fed to the newspaper — particularly the one about the women on Haycox's boat — and that Haycox had retaliated by having the note called.

If Van Auken had been surprised before, now he was stunned. The demand for payment made sense all of a sudden, in a chilling sort of way. He had not done what they accused him of.

Infuriated, he went to see Bruce Thompson.

At first, Thompson denied that he or Haycox had anything to do with the note being called. In the face of Van Auken's accusations, he finally capitulated.

"We thought it was you spreading the stories," he said, with a shrug, "but we've since found out it was someone else. I'm sorry this happened, but it's just one of those things."

Van Auken was livid.

"You almost destroyed me, my children and ruined a friendship between me and Ricky!" he shouted. "This is not a game!"

Thompson was apologetic, but said that what was done was done.

Van Auken explained to Franklin that he held no real animosity toward Haycox and Thompson.

"These guys got into a power thing being friends with Robb," he said. "But I was flabbergasted at what they did to me. We are sociable now and I still like them, but the trust necessary to be close friends will probably never be there again."

While the story Van Auken told was unsettling, it was not what Franklin was looking for. He still didn't have anyone who said they had used cocaine with Robb or had seen him use it. If Franklin didn't have that, he didn't have anything.

Chapter Nine

Fireworks on the Fourth of July

"The only person I have loved, emotionally or physically, is my bride, though, like any other red-blooded American, I have some fun from time to time."
Charles S. Robb, November 10, 1987, during his announcement that he would run for the Senate

As June 1988 wore on, right before things got ugly, Bill Franklin's phone was ringing off the hook with people who wanted to talk to him. Some had consciences of their own to ease; some had axes to grind, and admitted it. Some had already talked with Rose Ellen O'Connor; others had not.

All of them, it seemed, had stories to tell.

The Barfield Detective Agency provided guard service for Camp Pendleton, the Virginia Beach National Guard installation which adjoins Croatan, where the governor's official vacation residence is located. John Barfield, the agency's owner, came to Bill Franklin to say that he had checked their logs for the front gate. It was not unusual, Barfield said, for Robb to leave the camp around 10:30 p.m. and return the following morning around dawn.

Another story that was passed on to Bill Franklin concerned a man named John Bass. In the early 1980's, Bass was a small time drug dealer with connections to girls who liked to party. He also worked as a bartender at Summer's, a bar in the Ocean House Motel in Virginia Beach in which Bruce Thompson was a partner. A man who had been in jail with Bass told Franklin that Bass said that he had been approached by Thompson to provide drugs and girls for a party on one occasion when Robb came to town. Bass agreed, and attended the party himself.

Drugs, Bass said, were everywhere. And Robb had arrived with Thompson, as promised.

When Bass was later arrested on drug charges, he told his story to his attorney, hoping that some deal with the Commonwealth Attorney might be forthcoming. It was not.

Bill Franklin went to see Bass' attorney, Robert Morecock. Morecock confirmed that Bass had told him this story.

John Bass was living in California when Bill Franklin tracked him down. When Bass heard what Franklin was calling about, his tone was sharp.

"I've done my time," he snapped. "I've paid my dues for what I did. I left all that shit behind me and I'm turning my whole life around. Leave me alone. I don't want to get involved in that mess again."

Bass hung up.

A week after Franklin contacted Bass, a cop came to see Franklin. He was a big, tough, experienced, no-nonsense Virginia Beach police detective who had been working on assignment with the U.S. Customs Service in their drug enforcement division. The cop and Franklin went way back together, their paths cris-crossing during many years on cases.

"Bill," the cop said when he called at the end of June, "I've got someone I think you want to talk to. She's reliable and truthful. And she has some first hand information for you." "Bring her over," Franklin told him, "this weekend. Out to the house."

It was Fourth of July weekend, 1988. While most of the people in Virginia Beach were celebrating the holiday, Bill Franklin, the policeman and Becky Harris sat by Franklin's pool and talked.

Franklin found Harris attractive, well-educated, poised. Tall, blond, perfectly groomed, in her 30's, Harris exemplified the socially proper Virginia Beach look. She owned a high-fashion women's clothing store called Tres Chic.

The story Harris told began in 1982. With Harris' permission, Franklin taped the conversation.

A young woman named Tai Collins had worked for Harris part-time at Tres Chic and part-time as a lifeguard at the Woodbury Apartments, which Harris managed. In March 1982, Harris sponsored Collins in the Miss Virginia USA Pageant, which she won. As part of her official duties early that summer, Collins assisted in the dedication of Waterside, a new pavilion of shops and restaurants on the downtown Norfolk waterfront. Also on hand for the dedication was Governor Chuck Robb.

"After that meeting Chuck Robb would call my business and ask for Tai, or would call my home and ask to speak to Tai," Harris said. "And they got together. Chuck introduced Tai to Bruce Thompson who then became the mediator between Chuck, Tai and me."

The first party Harris went to with Collins and Robb was the birthday party for John Bennis, given by his wife Gina. It was held on the top of the Ocean Ranch Hotel. Harris estimated there were over 200 guests dancing around the pool and roaming through the rooms on the top floor that had been opened for the revelers. "There was food, drink, drugs, anything," Harris said. "You say drugs. What did you see?" Franklin asked her. "Pot, cocaine, uppers, downers, a mixture," she paused. "Anything you wanted. It was all over the place."

"Just laying out on the table?"

"Yeah, they had it laying out on the table in open view." Robb and Collins, like Bruce Thompson, Gene Schmidt, Marty Pallazio, Ed Ruffin and the other guests, were in and out of all the rooms during the course of the evening, Harris said.

Harris was uncomfortable in the presence of the drugs. "I told Tai 'I'm not staying. This is not a place I want to be, and I really don't think that it's a place you need to be'." Harris left alone.

"Tai," she said, "left later with Robb and his people."

Throughout the summer, Robb or Thompson continued to invite Collins and Harris to parties. In August, Bruce Thompson called Harris about a dinner party at his house.

"He read me off the guest list and said 'Chuck' and I said 'Well, all you're going to do is sit around and do drugs. . .if Tai wants to come that's her business.'"

Collins went to the party alone and called Harris at 2:00 a.m.

"She called me when she got home. . .said it was wild."

"What do you mean wild?" Franklin asked.

"That they were doing drugs and Chuck was wild. She said she left and came home."

While Collins and Harris were on the telephone, Robb showed up driving a jeep around in circles in the parking lot outside Collins' apartment. She finished her conversation with Harris saying that Robb wanted to go to the beach and that she was going with him.

At the end of the summer of 1982, Tai Collins moved to New York to pursue her modeling career.

Franklin asked Harris if Robb ever went to visit Collins in New York.

"Yes. She called and said he was coming up. She stayed with him at his hotel. She told me that."

Before they were finished, Franklin again asked Harris about the cocaine. Referring back to Bennis' birthday party, Franklin asked Harris, "There's no question in your mind that at the one party you went to. . .you don't do drugs, but you're aware of what drugs look like and what have you, and the governor was in and out of the same rooms you were. . .and these were just right out on the table. . .?"

"Right out on the table," Harris replied. "I mean everybody was standing around with it in containers, offering it and doing it, you know, they had their dollar bills rolled up real tight. . .."

"Did that appear to be rather unusual to you, for the governor to be there?" Franklin asked.

"Yes it did," Harris said emphatically.

"Anybody else?"

"No," she said, shaking her head, "because everyone gave me the impression that it was standard procedure. It was a party, you know, and they said that he came to these parties just like a regular guest."

Harris talked on, sketching the interactions in the party and drug scene in greater detail for Franklin, naming people who appeared at the parties that Robb frequented. All the names were familiar, the same names that pounded through Bill Franklin's head late at night: Thompson, Schmidt, Kern, Pallazio.

And Robb.

Chapter Ten

The Out-of-Towners

"One of the key things we did find out, organized crime members indeed were frequenting that area."
Robert L. Berryman, Director State Police Bureau of Criminal Investigations
The Virginian-Pilot and The Ledger-Star,
June 18, 1985

July is hot in Virginia Beach. The sun peeks up gently over the Atlantic Ocean, warming the sand. Tourists pay up to $200 a day for that view. Residents take it for granted.

By mid-day, that sun is unmerciful; its blinding noon-time light gives no quarter to the unprotected.

There are no shadows, little shade to hide in.

Bill Franklin is a guy who sweats a lot. The actual temperature often hardly seems to matter. Perspiration runs off his forehead in rooms that are comfortable to other people. Mid-summer is a bitch for Bill Franklin. It makes him sweat like hell.

His talk with Becky Harris left him reeling. It was yet another confirmation of Robb's proximity to cocaine and possible use of it and he had this talk on tape.

No one else knew what he was hearing from these people. His employees didn't know; Keetie didn't know. He was all alone with it.

People continued to come to him with stories to tell. One friend from the Virginia Beach Police Department came to Franklin during July 1988. During the summers of 1983 and 1984, the man had ridden with the city's mounted patrol and had often stopped at Bruce Thompson's Croatan residence to water his horse. On at least two of these stops, the man said, he had seen Chuck Robb acting "lovey dovey" with a blond woman.

Interesting, perhaps, but not particularly helpful. Robb's dalliances were well-known and, Franklin felt, not all that important. An extramarital affair, he pointed out, is not illegal. Cocaine is.

Before they parted, the man had another story he wanted to share with Franklin. It involved a "hit" on Eddie Garcia, the Virginia Beach businessman who had attended the Gargulio wedding in New York and who had been one of the targets of Operation Seagull.

The telephone call came from a cop in Newport News to a cop in Virginia Beach during the spring of 1987 around the time of the Richmond *Times-Dispatch* story connecting Chuck Robb to cocaine users.

The Newport News cop said he needed to check something out. "You got a guy over there, a well known guy maybe, a businessman? A guy with the name of. . .wait a minute. . .let me check. . .a guy with the name of Garcia?"

"Yeah," the Virginia Beach cop said, chuckling in understatement, "we got one of those."

"Well," the Newport News cop said, "somebody wants to kill him."

This was the policeman's story:

A man and a woman had driven to the Holiday Inn in Newport News at the end of a long day. The man settled the van in a parking space at the motel. They had neither need nor desire to rent a room, since the van was equipped with what they needed most at the moment, which was a place to make love. The weather was mild; they opened the sliding windows on the side of the van. The other reason they didn't want to rent a room was because they were married. But not to each other.

In the midst of their passion, they heard two cars pull alongside their van and then they heard voices. Startled, concerned, the man looked out the van window and listened.

One man was in a white Cadillac, two men were in the other car, also a luxury model, maybe a Lincoln Town car, he said later.

The man in the Cadillac started to explain to the other two men what needed to be done, which was that Eddie Garcia needed to be killed. Talking back and forth between the cars wasn't working, so the man in the Cadillac got out and walked to the passenger side of the other car. Now he was standing right beside the van.

The two men, dark and dispassionate, listened to the instructions and nodded their heads. Unbeknownst to them, the man in the van was listening too.

Money — the man in the van couldn't hear exact amounts — was discussed, a down payment to be made that day and the remainder to be paid after the job was taken care of. Something went from the Cadillac man's hand to the hand of one of the men in the other car. The man in the van believed it was a wad of cash. He was trembling as he wrote down the license number of the white Cadillac. The other car, with its unfamiliar New Jersey license plates, was out of sight before he could copy down all its numbers.

The man in the van slept fitfully that night. He had to tell someone what he had heard, but he could hardly explain in public what he happened to be doing in a van in a motel parking lot late in the afternoon with another man's wife. By the time dawn was breaking, he thought he had a solution to his dilemma. The Newport News cop was a friend of his. If anyone ever used his name in connection with the story, the man vowed, he would deny all of it. The Newport News cop said he'd pass the story on to the Virginia Beach police.

Eddie Garcia was most certainly a well known name in Virginia Beach and the surrounding cities of Hampton Roads. Federal, state and local authorities had spent 20 years and several million dollars investigating Garcia, a Norfolk native of Spanish descent, his businesses, his friends and associates. Garcia has acknowledged publicly that he is friendly with several organized crime figures, and that he was one of the primary targets of the Operation Seagull surveillance in 1980.

Garcia has never been charged with an offense involving organized crime. Garcia has been arrested only once and that was in July 1988, when he was charged with allegedly supplying poker machines to a gambling operation. The charge was later dismissed.

In fact, Garcia and developer John Aragona had received letters of apology from the city of Virginia Beach in 1976 after Aragona filed an harassment suit in connection with local police surveillance of his and Garcia's activities.

It did not seem out of the question to the Virginia Beach cop that someone might really want to kill Garcia. He thought it over briefly and went to Paul Sciortino, the Commonwealth's Attorney for Virginia Beach. By the time he did that, the Newport News police already knew who owned the Cadillac.

The white Cadillac was registered to an attorney who had often entertained Robb at his home. He told the officers that he had never been near the motel parking lot.

The few numbers that had been distinguishable on the New Jersey license plate were insufficient to trace that car.

Although he has lived in Virginia Beach for almost a quarter of a century, Paul Sciortino still bears some of the demeanor of the Brooklyn boy he once was, and much of the accent. A graduate of St. John's College, Sciortino first went to work for the FBI and then moved to Virginia Beach in 1970. He was elected Commonwealth's Attorney in 1981.

It was only logical that in that position he would come to know Eddie Garcia. It was, in some ways, as rumor after rumor about Garcia's alleged activities emerged and could not be proven, Sciortino and Garcia would become friends.

"I have to talk to you," Sciortino called Garcia. "Alone. I don't want anyone else there. This is very, very serious."

When he arrived at Garcia's oceanfront condominium, the two men went to a rear bedroom where their conversation would not be overheard.

Sciortino laid the story out for Garcia.

Garcia reacted at first with dumbfounded silence, paling at the news. When he spoke at last, it was Sciortino who was stunned.

"I know where it's coming from," Garcia said. "It's Robb's people. They think I'm the one spreading the rumors about the drugs."

Security officers lived with the Garcia family for a month, checking everyone entering the lobby in the condo building during the day and living in the family's quarters at night. Garcia arranged a personal meeting with Chuck Robb in Richmond where Robb was practicing law with the firm of Hunton and Williams. Their association extended back at least to 1982 when Garcia had contributed to Robb's gubernatorial campaign. During the ensuing years Garcia often provided limousines for Robb's use when he was in the area as well as a room at his Pavilion Hotel. However, Garcia had told Robb that he was no longer welcome there since his indiscreet behavior within the hotel had become impossible to ignore.

In the conversation, Garcia assured Robb that it was others — not he — who had been talking about Robb's presence at the beach parties. Robb denied that he knew anything about the alleged plan to kill Garcia and seemed appalled that anyone close to him would consider such an act. Garcia suggested that Robb spread the word to his underlings.

No harm has come to Garcia, and no charges were ever leveled against anyone.

Concerned for his own safety, Franklin contacted the Virginia Beach Police Chief, Charles Wall, in an attempt to verify the incident involving Garcia. Chief Wall offered no comment and referred Franklin to Captain Billy Deans of the Special Investigative Unit. Deans refused to confirm or deny the story and flatly refused to discuss the matter.

Franklin then realized that he could not expect to receive any help from the top brass at the Virginia Beach Police Department.

Months later, Franklin discovered that Detective J.O. "Taco" Williamson of the Newport News Police Department had taken the call from the man in the van and had personally contacted a detective at the Virginia Beach Police Department.

Detective Williamson told Franklin that the facts he had concerning the attempted "hit" on Garcia were indeed correct. Williamson also told Franklin that once he passed the information on to Virginia Beach, the investigators from that police department handled the case thereafter.

Chapter Eleven

Midsummer Pressure

"I'm damned if I do and damned if I don't in this case."
          Bill Franklin, *The Danville Register*

The first tentative whispers of fear entered Bill Franklin's consciousness after hearing the Garcia story. He wasn't exactly scared — hell, not much scares him — but this investigation was going further than he ever expected and it was taking him into something that was beginning to feel almost bottomless.

He was beginning to not like it at all.

By the middle of July 1988, the phones at Franklin Security Systems were ringing like crazy as word of Bill Franklin's on-going investigation spread. People he had known and worked with for 20 years and more wanted to talk to Bill about his investigation of Robb. Bill, they said, why don't you just quit it, leave it alone? They weren't swayed by his insistence that it was a legitimate job, that he was fair. They didn't care; just stop doing it, they said.

In the midst of it all, two of his biggest clients canceled their contracts for pre-employment polygraph tests which were the mainstay of Franklin's business.

Franklin noticed that for all the calls that were coming in to dissuade him from continuing, there was also an eerie silence from people he thought were friends who weren't calling so much anymore. And when he went into any of the Virginia Beach bars that he'd frequented so regularly over the years, an almost imperceptible hush seemed to fall. There were lots and lots of empty seats around him.

He was going to be increasingly friendless through this, he realized, and poorer, too, if his clients were being pressured to quit him. The worst of it, he thought, was that it was affecting everyone around him, especially the women who were closest to him. No one in Franklin's proximity was going to be able to escape the stress that was building and spilling over into his personal and professional life.

He hadn't built Franklin Security Systems by himself. He had the help of three women, all different, each strong in her own way: Keetie, his wife; Diane Heaney, his top investigator; and Cindy Upson, his secretary and office manager. All three of them had been through a lot with him over the years. And he had a daughter, too, whose life would obviously be affected by his investigation.

Now, he had put them all at risk. Was it worth the risk to continue to pursue Chuck Robb? And was it fair for him to drag the women for whom he cared so deeply into it? Was this what they had all worked so hard for?

When Bill Franklin left Falls Church, Virginia, in 1963 to open the new business in Norfolk and Virginia Beach, he left his bride of three years, Keetie, behind. During those first two years, he commuted weekly between Norfolk and Falls Church. It meant hard work and long hours and it was lonely — Bill slept on a cot in the new office — but Keetie was as determined as he to make their life successful.

Bill Franklin met Marquitta "Keetie" Klein at the wedding of a mutual friend in Washington, D.C. in December 1959. Bill was a last-minute stand-in in the wedding party; they picked him because the tuxedo would fit. At the reception, a wedding guest pointed toward a young woman across the room.

"There's a girl you ought to get to know," he said. The girl with the dark hair and brown eyes was a microbiologist from Maryland. Their attraction was immediate. They were engaged after two weeks and married within three months.

The early years were not always easy, but they had fun, the kind of endearing and enduring fun that is a necessary underpinning of a successful marriage.

From the beginning, Keetie worked with Bill as his bookkeeper but kept herself out of his cases, the two of them forming a near-perfect yin and yang for business success: he as the quintessential front man, working the crowd, and Keetie, in the background, managing the money. The success kept coming. At first, Bill and Keetie Franklin seem to be polar opposites. Bill blusters into a room, all bulk and voice and presence; Keetie is quieter, soft spoken. Talk with them awhile, though, and underneath the exteriors they present to the world at large are values, views and attitudes that mesh almost perfectly. On the 100-acre farm where Keetie grew up, self-sufficiency was the first rule of life. Her parents, both German, required strict obedience and considered procrastination and laziness to be the two worst sins.

Procrastination and laziness are virtually foreign to Bill Franklin. "Do it, do it now, and do it well" are his guidelines. "Bill Franklin could never tolerate indifference," Keetie says. The whirlwind courtship seems less surprising: they spoke to one another in the common language of excellence and drive from their first meeting.

They each came from families where there had been open discord and, from that, they share a dislike of it. They argue rarely, fight even less. Even though their styles of upset are different, they are complementary. He blows quick and loud, theatrical. When the steam is blown off, he subsides and all is calm again. Where Bill is all projection and high drama, Keetie is controlled. She keeps close counsel on her anger, mulls it over, lets it build. But when a flush steals up from her neck to her fair Germanic face, those around her know to run. It doesn't happen often, but when she has had enough, her upset can go on for a day or two.

Keetie gave birth to their only child, Donna, in Fairfax, in 1963. She was working at the Food and Drug Administration and Bill was commuting from Norfolk. Donna saw her father so seldom during those first years that she called her baby sitter's husband "Daddy."

From her first day of school, Donna remembers, it was drilled into her that education was the key to everything, the way out and up, the only way out and up. Grades were of utmost importance and report card days were critical. She always did well.

Diane Heaney and Cindy Upson know about the Franklins' determination from first hand experience. Each had been with Bill Franklin for nearly 20 years by the time the Robb investigation dramatized an already-exciting line of work. When she first came to work for Bill Franklin, Diane was in her 20's, blond, petite, seemingly an unlikely candidate for a business traditionally built on macho.

But her background was hardly cream-puff. She was a self-described "tough kid" and her street smarts seemed to be built-in. And she was a natural for the business of private investigations.

She was as good in her domain at Franklin Security Systems as Bill Franklin was at his. Diane handled the pre-employment psychological testing that the company did and she was in charge of all domestic investigations. In addition, she ran polygraph examinations — she studied in one of Bill's classes — and is a crackerjack interrogator.

Like Diane, Cindy Upson, Bill's secretary and office manager, personifies the sense of dedication that Bill Franklin holds so dear. Soft spoken, efficient, she is a rock of solidity, calm and kindness. She is perfectly content to let her co-workers go out on the streets and live the drama. She'd rather hear their stories than be part of them.

Just because she's not out working cases doesn't mean that Cindy's life is mundane. Far from it. Bill Franklin is a self-admitted son of a bitch to work for. He's demanding. He wants everything done yesterday. Or two days ago. And no mistakes. Perfection is not too much to strive for.

Of all the people around him, Cindy is probably the most sensitive to his outbursts, but over the course of two decades she has come to accept Franklin's intensity and to consider it all part of a day's work.

As that first summer of the Robb investigation was waning, Cindy, perhaps even more than the other employees, realized how seriously the business was being affected by Franklin's investigation of Robb; she knew that there were clients, big clients, who weren't calling anymore. She knew that there were friends who used to call to say hello to Bill who weren't calling either.

"Even if I hadn't known what it was," she recalled, "I would have known that something was going on. You could really feel the changes in the business and see the changes in Bill. He looked so tired and worried all the time."

At home, Keetie saw the changes too. All these years, all this faith, all this goodness: she'd never been scared for him before. But in the mornings, when he left the house, she could not help but feel the breath of fear all about her. He'd never talked to her about his cases anyway, but this time his silence was worse. She could see all she needed to know behind his eyes. The house was safe, of course. The sophisticated alarm system, the fence, and the two big dogs, Smokey and Sheba, made the Franklin home an enclave of safety.

Bill Franklin tried to tell himself that there was really nothing to worry about, that everything would turn out fine. Even if he couldn't rely on the continued support of friends and business associates, he could rely on the women in his life to be there for him, to take care of his home and his business. They cared about him enough to stand by him no matter what happened.

He thought back through the investigation and realized that July had started off with his interview with Rebecca Harris and then barely a week later the information about the hit on Eddie Garcia came to him.

The month was only half over and he was tired and wary.

They threatened to kill Bill Franklin for the first time on July 13, 1988.

Chapter Twelve

Risky Business

"A private investigator hired to check into persistent rumors linking U.S. Senate nominee Charles Robb with Virginia Beach drug trafficking has received two threats on his life."

The Washington Times

The first death threat came while Keetie was away from home at a funeral in Maryland. When Bill saw the answering machine light flashing in the kitchen, he hoped that it was she who had called.

He didn't recognize the man's voice, but his words were exceedingly clear.

"If you want to stay alive, quit messing with. . .Stop!" Franklin glared down at the answering machine and played the message again.

"You son of a bitch!" he howled. "You son of a bitch! Not in my own home!"

Four days later, it happened again.

Billy Carroll was the captain of Franklin's charter boat, the "Top Hook." On Saturday, July 17, he was readying the boat for a charter group when the phone rang. The male caller asked for Bill Franklin.

"He's not on board," Carroll answered.

"Then give him a message," the caller growled. "You tell Bill Franklin that he is a dead motherfucker."

Carroll was terrified. He called Bill Franklin at once. "It wasn't what the guy said, boss. It was how he sounded. This guy was real, real serious."

Bill Franklin thought about it for a long time. He was furious beyond belief; he was also troubled. Usually people who make phone threats are cowards who don't have the balls to threaten you to your face. This time, he felt, was different. A pattern of intimidation was emerging. The clients, the social snubs, and now death threats all seemed intended to make him quit the Robb case after only six weeks of investigating. Was it really that important? Was it really possible that someone would try to kill him to get this investigation to stop? How far would they go?

His years of experience told him that there was nothing the police could do to protect him and that he couldn't actually prove that all of this was related to the Robb investigation. Still, he wanted the death threats on the record.

He went to the Virginia Beach police.

Chapter Thirteen

The P.I. and the Police

"When the police wanted a killer to sing, they called in Billy A. Franklin, private eye, to help him recall the tune."

The Virginian-Pilot and The Ledger-Star

Bill Franklin was no stranger to the police departments in Norfolk and Virginia Beach, and he numbered scores of officers and administrators among his friends. Their professional respect for him was enormous, prompting then-detective and now Virginia Beach Sheriff Frank Drew to call him the "only private detective that I know of who the police will cooperate with 100 percent." They cooperate with him because he gets the job done. Franklin was a pioneer in the state of Virginia in the use of the polygraph in investigations.

Although it was in the Army's Counter-Intelligence Corps that Franklin first learned the valuable tricks of what would become his trade, such as interrogation and surveillance, what he really wanted to learn was the polygraph. But the Army wouldn't send him to polygraph school unless he agreed to re-enlist. In 1961, he left the Army and went to polygraph school in New York on his own money and his own time. It may have been the smartest time and money he ever spent.

Franklin's use of the sometimes controversial polygraph test became the financial underpinning for the rapid growth of Franklin Security Systems. He opened his first private investigative company in northern Virginia with a friend who was a former police officer. After a falling out between the two men three years later, Franklin went out on his own and relocated to Hampton Roads.

Among the first things he did was to open the Virginia School of Polygraph.

It comes as no surprise to anyone who knows him that Bill Franklin holds Polygraph License No. 1 in the state of Virginia. His campaign for licensing of all polygraph examiners began in 1962, when use of the instrument was as yet unregulated. With his lobbying, a measure passed the state House but not the state Senate that year. In 1966, a bill was passed but it was not stringent enough to suit Franklin. In 1974, a tough, amended bill went through, and its provisions included establishing a strict advisory board. Franklin served on the Polygraph Examiners Board from 1974 until 1986.

Franklin made legal history in Virginia when he testified as an expert witness in a robbery and shooting trial in 1976 in which the defendant, Van Burton, was given a life sentence after being found guilty as a result of Franklin's testimony.

It was the first time in the state of Virginia that a conviction rested on the testimony of a polygraph expert. It was also the first of many times that a criminal would be sorry to run up against Bill Franklin or one of the hundreds of polygraph examiners he trained.

When Carl R. Chalmers, a 27-year-old paint maker, was a suspect in the murder and rape of 13-year-old Lou Ann Byars, it was Bill Franklin who elicited a confession. The police brought Chalmers to Franklin after a police-administered polygraph test proved inconclusive.

The test that Franklin administered clearly indicated that Chalmers was lying. Franklin confronted the tall, bearded man in his best, fatherly "you can talk to me" manner.

"Before it was all over," Franklin recalls, "we were both cryin'. Sittin' there with tears streaming down our faces. I knew he wanted to get it off his chest. Sometimes you just have to give them the space to do it."

Sometimes police officers helped him as well. One of the most often-told stories holds all the classic suspense elements: Bill Franklin as the quintessential private eye, a city police detective willing to take a big risk, a high-speed chase, a good-looking woman, a secret money drop, a clandestine charter flight to Florida and a missing brief-case with more than $100,000 in it. They left in the middle of the night. For the first and only time, Bill wouldn't even tell Keetie where he was going, just that he'd been hired to do a job and he'd be back in a day, maybe two. He named the detective who was going with him, just to let her know he wouldn't be alone.

The only thing they told the pilot of the plane they chartered was to head south. Hours later, they told him the name of the small town in Florida they were going to. They didn't care where they landed, they said. They just needed to be close. A sleepy-eyed security guard was dozing in his car when the small plane began to circle the grassy runways of the tiny airport in the dead of night. They landed by the light of the guard's high beams.

The cash-filled briefcase they'd gone to retrieve belonged to a man in Virginia Beach. It had been officially reported to the police as a theft of $2,500 in order to avoid questions about the actual large sum of money. It was, without a doubt, the kind of case somebody would shoot you for.

The airport security guard drove the two men to the house where the money was said to be hidden. He dropped them off, but alerted the local police because they seemed to be such unsavory characters.

In a scene reminiscent of the Keystone Cops, Franklin and his cohort were picked up by the police and taken to the station house. In a scene further reminiscent of almost impossible coincidence, the desk sergeant at the precinct they were taken to recognized Franklin at once. They had attended a seminar together.

Released after they explained their mission in general terms, Franklin and the detective returned to the house. The occupant, who began to scream loudly in the belief that they had come to kill him, was quick to strike a deal in which the money would be brought to them at a certain location at a certain time. Enter the good looking woman, who was to be part of the drop plan. Enter, too, the speeding car from which a sackful of money was thrown into bushes near the appointed spot, but not so close that Bill saw it go. Leaving his partner behind, Franklin set off in hot pursuit.

When he gave up the chase and returned to the drop spot, his partner had the cash firmly in hand.

Mission accomplished. Fee earned. Another story added to the Franklin legend.

Sgt. Ken Boner and Lt. Frank Drew met Franklin at the second precinct on a summer night in 1988. They'd both known Franklin for decades. They listened to his story of the death threat. They believed him. And it scared them both.

"Goddamit, Bill," Drew berated him, "I can't believe you're not carrying your gun."

In spite of the fact that he'd had a concealed weapons permit for 30 years, Bill Franklin had carried his gun twice in ten years, and those times only because the cases specifically required it. He hated the idea of it, hated these anonymous voices for forcing him to it.

After he met with Boner and Drew, he put his shoulder holster on every morning when he dressed for the day. The .38 Smith & Wesson thumped against him all day long. Its presence reminded him, nagged at him, pissed him off.

Nothing, he thought, was ever going to be the same.

News travels fast within the law enforcement community. It was hardly a surprise, then, when a friend from a Police Department 50 miles away in Henrico County heard about the death threats and showed up at his office a week later.

He brought Franklin a present.

"Don't take any chances, Bill," the man said as he handed Franklin a brand new bulletproof vest, still in its box. "Wear it."

Franklin thanked him, and said he would take his advice. When the man left, Bill Franklin stared at the box.

"Point Blank Body Armor," it read. The fine print on the white jacket assured the wearer that it was rated to protect against .357 Magnum, 9 mm "and lesser threats."

Bill Franklin packed the protection back into its box. He'd carry a gun, but he'd be damned if he was going to put that vest on every day.

For the first time, a chill of real fear made its presence known and Bill Franklin said yes to it.

"Yes," he said, "I know you're there. Yes, goddamit, if the cops who've known me all these years are scared for me, I'd be a complete idiot not to be scared too."

He tried to remember being scared before so he could remember how he handled it then. There had been so few times; fear did not come to him easily. And those times had all been situational: an infuriated husband caught in flagrante with his mistress; a client's employee coming in for a polygraph over an inside theft; the basic psychos of the world who seemed ready to flip out in a bar fight.

This was different and he knew it. It felt different inside his belly. This was worse, this was bigger, this seemed to go in many directions and deep.

It had all happened so quickly! The investigation wasn't even two months old.

"Well," he thought, "quitting is out of the question. Would he allow himself to be intimidated by anyone? Hell no. Who the hell did they think he was?"

The only thing to do, he realized, was to scare the bastards right back.

He couldn't prove anything then, can't prove it now. But he went back to talk to a couple of the people he'd talked to originally and he told them this:

"If you mess with me or my family or my employees, I guarantee you there will be trouble, I mean trouble, like no one has ever seen around here. And you better fuckin' spread the word wherever it needs to be spread."

His warning apparently sunk in and was passed along. It was a year before they threatened to kill him again.

Chapter Fourteen

Frankie and Jamie

*"Chuck Robb has been buoyed up by women, but
he may be brought down by them too."*
Regardie's Magazine, October 1990

Frankie and Jamie were whores. Their names and sexual talents were well known throughout the Virginia Beach party community in the mid-1980's. For $200 each, you could have them for the night. A birthday party, a bachelor party, a big party or a very private party: it really didn't matter. If you met their price, they'd be there. If you had cocaine to offer in addition to cash, that was even better.

"Frankie" and "Jamie" were professional names they had chosen for themselves. Frankie was born Vicki Ann Wheeless in Philadelphia in 1962. At 5'8", she was the taller of the two, and thin, with long brown hair. Jamie was older — she turned 31 in 1986 — blond, and shorter. Her real name was Margo Maureen Cassano.

When people talked to Bill Franklin about the parties at the beach where cocaine and Chuck Robb had coincided, they talked about Frankie and Jamie too. There were times, they said, when Frankie and Jamie were the entertainment for Robb and his friends, servicing them openly.

Franklin had been looking for Frankie and Jamie since May, putting the word out that he wanted to talk to them. No one seemed to know where they might be. The word on the street was that they had gone to New Jersey.

Preston Berry Jr., the president of Security Technology International, a security firm with offices in Norfolk and in Florida, knew Frankie and Jamie during the summer of 1986. He had hired the women on the occasion of a friend's birthday party, and Berry, a bachelor in 1986, had befriended the women on occasion. They felt they could trust him.

Berry had heard that Bill Franklin was looking for the women. In July 1988, he came to Franklin with the following story:

One night in July 1986, Jamie called Preston at home. She was stuck, she said, in a bad situation at Croatan. Could Berry, she asked, come get her? She gave him the address.

Jamie was waiting in front of Bruce Thompson's house when Preston pulled up in his Trans Am. She was scared and upset when she got into the car, and asked Berry to wait to see if her girlfriend was coming out also. After waiting a few minutes, Berry took Jamie home.

She was too upset that night to talk much, Berry said, but was able to tell him that someone had come to the house to sell drugs, the deal had been made and then there had been an argument. Several weeks later she told him the whole story of that night and others.

"She was basically boasting and bragging about the point of being with the governor of the state. . .," Berry said.

"Talking about Chuck Robb?" Franklin asked.

"Chuck Robb," Berry affirmed. "That she had been at parties where he was, and she had been with some other celebrities. . .. She was telling me about several times that she had been at other parties with a girl named Frankie, which was her girlfriend, one of her partners when they asked for two girls, that they had taken turns on the same individual which was Chuck Robb."

"Taking turns doing what?"

"Taking turns as far as being sexual with him," Berry replied.

Later that same summer, Jamie called on her friend Preston again. He picked the two women up at the Beach Cabaret on the oceanfront and took them to dinner.

They were scared, they told him, scared they were getting in too deep with some of the important people around the beach. Frankie had been arrested for soliciting at a party and the Virginia Beach police were leaning on both of them about giving information on others, offering to dismiss the charges against Frankie.

"They wanted to know what I would recommend for them to do since they trusted me," Berry told Franklin.

"Were they a little afraid of these prominent people?" Franklin asked.

"Yes," Berry said, "they were. They were afraid not only of the police on one side, but of the prominent people on the other side. So, they really didn't want to go forward to the police and give them information, because they were more afraid of the prominent people than they were of the police."

"Can't say I blame them," Franklin said, with no small hint of irony.

Frankie and Jamie told Berry about the parties they had been paid to attend, parties on boats where Thompson, Ricky Haycox, Ed Ruffin and Chuck Robb were among those present.

Cocaine, the women told him, was plentiful at every gathering they had ever gone to with these people, and sex was wide open.

"You said that Jamie said there was a whole lot of fucking, sucking and snorting coke?" Franklin asked.

"That is absolutely correct," Berry replied.

"And that included the governor?"

"That is correct," Berry said. "She said that there was cocaine at every party that she ever went to, and that it was plentiful."

"I think you indicated to me that she had said that Governor Robb had been doing cocaine like everybody else."

"Just like everybody else at the party," Berry said.

Chapter Fifteen

Stirring the Pot

"But no one counted on Franklin's absurd tenacity."

Regardie's Magazine October 1990

While the information from Preston Berry didn't particularly shock Bill Franklin, it did leave him feeling profoundly unsettled. He began to feel tainted himself just by his proximity to the stories.

And while he'd heard so many stories of wild sex from so many people who had been at parties that he was almost becoming enured to it, the level of decadence that was being portrayed made him ill. The investigation heated up along with the summer. Franklin's network of friends, police officers, and informants was working for him like an efficient hive of bees, even as the stress inside of him was building up like a small but rumbling volcano.

And he was all alone with his information.

In another part of town, news reporter Rose Ellen O'Connor was not alone. Throughout the summer of 1988, she was in near-constant contact with her editors at *The Virginian-Pilot and The Ledger-Star* about the Robb story. She knew that she and Franklin were working the same beat, talking to many of the same people, and hearing many of the same stories.

Among the people to whom both spoke was a boat captain who had been invited to a fund-raising party for Robb in 1981. The party was held on a piece of then-vacant property and given by Ricky Dunnington as a political rally for Chuck Robb, then running for governor. Croatan was not yet developed. Only a few houses dotted the land.

A huge crowd of supporters gathered at the site where a tent had been set up and Dunnington's new "Sea Raven" had been pulled up to the dock.

There was a live band, and music rang out over the water. The boat captain made his way to the "Sea Raven," to look it over. He had been specifically invited by Ricky Dunnington, but was not a regular in the crowd.

There were several people on the deck, none of whom the man recognized. He made his way toward the cabin of the big boat. Inside the cabin, a group of men and women had lines of cocaine laid out. They were high, apparently from cocaine, and laughing.

He backed away from the cabin and left the boat.

He was, he said later, horrified that cocaine had been part of a political fund raising event.

The man was even more concerned about what he had seen when he had first gone on board: Chuck Robb had come out of the cabin and was stepping off the boat.

When the boat captain realized cocaine was being used, he left the party.

Although he heard the rumors concerning Robb and drugs throughout the ensuing years, he never talked about what he had seen.

Years later, his name surfaced during Rose Ellen O'Connor's investigation for her newspaper story. Although the man talked with O'Connor, he explained carefully that he had not actually seen Robb using cocaine and could only place him at the party and aboard the boat where he had, indeed, seen cocaine.

As O'Connor and Franklin intensified their investigation, the man began to receive numerous hang-up calls on his answering machine. Finally, a call came while he was at home.

The male voice on the other end of the phone was distinct and clear, the words unmistakable.

"Keep your mouth shut and quit talking to that newspaper woman or you're liable to end up dead," the voice said.

The level of paranoia and fear within the protective circle around Robb had risen so much that even people who had no clear cut evidence to offer Franklin or the press, other than to place Robb at a party where cocaine was being used, presented a distinct threat.

Like Franklin, O'Connor was "almost amazed," she said later, at the willingness of people to talk about the most intimate details of their lives. While Franklin was focusing on proving or disproving Robb's involvement with cocaine, O'Connor set her sights on the women who were part of the fast lane crowd, young women in their teens and early 20's who were treated with what one observer called "a plantation mentality": their role was to service the men, to be used and used up by men twice their age. By the summer of 1988, some of the women who had been part of the scene were heavily addicted to cocaine, still living in the shabby beach cottages to which they had gone home just a few years earlier after glittering parties at Croatan with Thompson, Ruffin, Kern, Haycox, Schmidt, Pallazio and Robb.

Older, not much wiser, their lives had deteriorated or, at the least, stayed static while the men who had paid many of them to come to parties, have sex and do drugs had grown wealthier, unscathed.

O'Connor tracked Frankie and Jamie to New Jersey, where they were staying in a cheap motel near the prison in which Jamie's husband, Paul, was serving time for drugs. The women confirmed that they were at the parties, they confirmed that they had been paid by Bruce Thompson, and they confirmed that they had been introduced to Chuck Robb.

When O'Connor asked the prostitutes if it was true that they had performed oral sex on Robb in a hot tub at Virginia Beach, Frankie said, "No comment."

It was no secret that Franklin and O'Connor were each conducting investigations into Robb's activities. Robb hired an attorney to act as his local counsel in Hampton Roads in order to monitor the newspaper's investigation and Rose Ellen O'Connor's conduct during her interviews.

At the same time, Bill Franklin's employees saw the changes that gradually deepened the lines in his face. He had decided from the beginning to keep this investigation to himself, not to implicate the others. Although he thought it would be over quickly, he had known from the outset that it would be sensitive. He had no idea how big it would get, how long it would take, how dangerous it might be. By July he was glad he had decided to keep his findings to himself.

The notes from his interviews, the tape recordings, and the ever-growing file folder traveled with him everywhere; they were never out of his sight or possession.

He told his staff about the death threats, gathered them together and explained about the phone calls as perfunctorily as he could. He didn't want to scare them, he said, but anyone close to him needed to know this much now.

The front door to the office, the one that had been unlocked even after hours when they'd sit around to have a drink and talk about their day's work together, was now always locked at five o'clock. If there was another truck or car on the street, one that none of them recognized, they'd watch it carefully. And no one left the office alone. Someone always watched them go. But no matter how stressful it became, Bill Franklin remained unrelenting. Every day and most nights he went out on the streets and into the bars and into the homes and wherever the people were who would talk to him.

In the middle of August, he drove to Loretto, Pennsylvania. Billy O'Dell had some things he wanted to talk about.

Chapter Sixteen

Mapping Out the Territory

"O'Dell said that cocaine use was widespread at the social functions and that he was surprised to see the governor in attendance."
The Virginian-Pilot and The Ledger-Star
August 28, 1988

Bill Franklin had watched Billy O'Dell grow up. Nothing in that now-distant past hinted at this present; no one could have predicted that this son of a Navy chief, solidly middle class, one-time ball boy for the Virginia Squires professional basketball team, would end up serving a seven-year sentence for distribution of cocaine, the only one of the crowd to do any heavy time. Success had come to him as a stockbroker, and as a restaurateur. He had the solid good looks, strong physique, and native intelligence of a man who could have life his way.

By 1987, he had trashed it all for cocaine.

Loretto Federal Prison is a minimum security facility, 30 miles west of Altoona, Pennsylvania, nestled in the mountains. The prison property adjoins the campus of St. Francis College. If a person has to serve time in prison, Loretto is not the worst place to do it.

By 1985, Billy O'Dell was at the heart of the cocaine distribution, use and parties in Virginia Beach. Federal drug agents had been investigating him for three years before his arrest in March 1987.

Like the others who were involved in cocaine — whether they were arrested or not — Billy O'Dell's life was not lived in a vacuum. The ripples of his ruin spread out to include other victims. For O'Dell, one of those victims was his mother, Mary. Until he was arrested, Mary O'Dell thought that she had a near-perfect son. He'd completed college with a Bachelor's degree from Virginia Wesleyan College.

He'd found success in business. He was attentive, caring. The shock of discovering the truth about his life was almost more than Mary could stand. A month after her only son's arrest, Mary O'Dell suffered a stroke. Her doctor said it was directly attributable to the stress. Three years later, the damage from her stroke lingers. She is frail and her speech is seriously impaired. There is financial strain on her as well. When Billy calls her — which he continues to do frequently — he calls collect. His guilt is enormous. Unlike many of the others who were drawn into the web of drugs and intrigue, O'Dell seems to feel genuine remorse. Huddled in the corner of a conference room at Loretto that summer day, Billy O'Dell took Bill Franklin's note pad and pen and, sketching quickly, he drew out the route the cocaine took as it made its way into all the pretty places and all the pretty people.

He placed himself at the top of the cluster, in a square box that he labeled "ME."

Arrows and lines connected the circles and boxes below him, stemming off from the four key players on the level immediately below his name. The four included fellow restaurateurs and others, some of whom had already faced drug indictments.

Like any good organizational chart, each man had several other names emerging beneath. Lines connected lawyers, builders, businessmen, other restaurateurs, and several young women — a veritable cross-section of the Virginia Beach business and social communities.

"That's it," O'Dell said as he finished sketching and handed the notebook back to Franklin. "This is how it happened."

After he had drawn the diagram, Billy O'Dell told the stories.

Summer 1983. Jungle Falls was a tourist-oriented recreational park on General Booth Boulevard at the southernmost end of the resort area. Owned by Eddie Garcia, Jungle Falls was a popular attraction for out-of-towners, and locally noted for its towering gorilla, named Hugh-Mongus, standing out in front. William Gooch, a one-time stockbroker who had also gone into the more lucrative business of dealing cocaine, rented Jungle Falls in order to hold a benefit to raise money for the Virginia Beach Rescue Squad.

Almost 1,000 people attended the event, the highlight of which was a "Tarzan and Jane" costume contest. Among the guests was the group that included Steve Arcese, Bruce Thompson, Marty Pallazio, Gene Schmidt, and Ricky and Bobby Dunnington. The judge for the Tarzan and Jane contest was Governor Charles Robb.

Cocaine and marijuana were everywhere, being used openly. "A person would have had to have been blind," O'Dell said, "not to see what was going on."

The winner of the Jane portion of the costume contest was a good-looking, well-built blond by the name of "K.K.". As the big party was winding down, word went out that the party would continue on — smaller, quieter, far more private — at Gene Schmidt's Croatan home.

Two state troopers drove Governor Robb to the party where O'Dell and his girlfriend, Thompson, Schmidt, Pallazio and the Dunnington brothers were already gathering. "K.K.", the newly-crowned "Jane" look-a-like, arrived with Robb.

Almost all the men at Schmidt's house had cocaine in their pockets. The drinking had started much earlier at Jungle Falls. By the time the group gathered at Croatan, O'Dell and Robb had been drinking straight vodka together for several hours.

At the height of the party, Thompson and Schmidt came to O'Dell with a problem. They'd run out of cocaine, they said. Could he share some of his?

O'Dell agreed and went into the bathroom where he laid out five good sized lines of coke on the counter. He was curious about whether or not the governor would partake, so he stood outside the bathroom door in the hallway.

Robb entered the bathroom alone, was inside for a few minutes, then left.

O'Dell went in immediately.

Two of the five lines were gone.

When O'Dell left the party around 2:30 in the morning, the party was still going strong inside the house. Robb and "K.K." had become a couple on the beach.

During that same summer of 1983, Fourth of July was celebrated at Ray Parsons' house at the North End of Virginia Beach. The parties at Parsons' house were legendary in those days for the amount of cocaine he made available to his guests. Chuck Robb arrived around two o'clock in the afternoon, with his wife and one of his daughters. The family stayed for several hours, while things were still fairly calm, and then departed. Around sundown, Robb returned alone in an unmarked state police car, escorted by two state troopers.

The party had begun to break loose by that time. As Robb emerged from the car, O'Dell noticed that "Cocaine Pete" Argenziano, O'Dell's cocaine courier from New York, and Ray Parsons were hanging over the balcony, laughing and carrying on. Argenziano and Parsons, high as kites on cocaine, had straws up their noses so they looked like walruses. They were waving to the governor as he arrived.

O'Dell was terrified about the two men being so obvious with the state police around. No one else seemed concerned.

The state troopers, members of the Executive Protection Detail, dropped Robb off and left. The party, like the others at Parsons' house, went on long into the night.

Bill Franklin thanked O'Dell for meeting with him. On the long ride back to Virginia, he thought about what he'd heard. The presence of the state troopers at these parties was troubling, but Franklin knew that the members of the state's Executive Protection Detail were sworn to absolute secrecy, and that state police answer directly to the governor of the Commonwealth. The members of the governor's detail are the cream of the crop; on the rare occasions that there is a vacancy or that the detail is being expanded to include more members, ten troopers will be interviewed for each one who is chosen.

They are selected based on their suitability for the job, and that suitability includes appearance, social graces, table manners and discretion as well as the ability to protect the governor, at whose pleasure they serve, from any harm. It is a position somewhat similar to the one Robb held as a young Marine at the Johnson White House.

"I think those guys take a blood oath," one state police source said later. "They don't talk to anybody about what they see or hear. I heard that the word went out in those days that they weren't to say anything to anybody unless they were called into court."

Another former state trooper agreed, and added, "Their job is to protect the governor. That means to protect him from anything and everything. From physical harm. From crowds. From the media. And, if necessary, from the law. Their job is not enforcement. It's protection."

It was no wonder, then, Franklin thought, that having state police around was no deterrent to the party-goers. As long as Robb was with them, they were safe.

Billy O'Dell was the closest thing to an eyewitness to Robb using cocaine that Bill Franklin had thus far; and O'Dell could only affirm that he had put down five lines, that Robb had been in the room alone, and that two lines had disappeared.

It was good, but not good enough.

Franklin knew he had a lot more people to talk to.

When Robert Melton called from *The Washington Post* several days later in August, Cindy put the call through and Franklin thought nothing about it. By now he had become accustomed to the calls from reporters who were covering the once-whispered rumors, and he took everyone of them, polite and helpful.

And he never gave them a thing they didn't already have. "Mr. Franklin," Melton said, "I'd like to get a comment from you regarding the complaint that the Robb for

Senate campaign has filed with the Federal Election Commission."

"What the hell are you talking about?" Franklin boomed. Melton was clearly surprised that he was the one breaking the news to Franklin.

"It's a complaint naming a John Doe as your employer and respondent to the suit," Melton said, "alleging that your investigation is clearly politically motivated and that, as such, your fee should be reported as a campaign expenditure or in-kind contribution to Robb's opponent, Maurice Dawkins."

"I have no comment to make," Bill Franklin said, "since I haven't the foggiest idea what the hell this is about."

Franklin knitted his fingers together on the top of the massive desk in his office and stared through the thin layer of smoke that perpetually hangs there. Once upon a time, this room had been the carport of this house-cum-office; once upon a time there had been nothing here. Now the walls around him were covered with plaques and awards and acknowledgements of his career; the room was a shrine to the work he had done, the man he had become.

His brain was reeling. Federal Election Commission? What the hell did he know about that? Not a damned thing, he thought. What did it mean, whom should he call, what in the name of Christ was he supposed to do now?

The room was hot; he was sweating. He was mad, he was confused, he was in over his head.

The only person he could think of who might conceivably have knowledge of federal election laws and the commission was William "Buster" O'Brien, a personal friend, former delegate to the General Assembly and an unsuccessful Republican candidate for Attorney General.

Franklin decided he would wait. Wait and see what would happen now. Maybe Melton was wrong; maybe this was some sort of con. He hadn't received anything from anyone or any commission; he would just wait until he did.

As he rose to leave his desk, his eyes fell on the far corner of the glass top. Amidst all the stacks of papers,

Billy Franklin in his office

Billy and Keetie

Tai Collins,
former Miss
Virginia—U.S.A.

Washington Post reporter
Don Baker

Ricky Chaplain, in front of Pavilion Athletic Club

Ricky Chaplain

Becky Harris

Courtney Cromwe

Virginia Beach Sheriff Frank Drew

Lewis H. Williams

Preston Berry, Jr., Security Technology International

Lt. Gary Van Auken

Cottage at Croatan Beach

The "Sea Raven," owned by the Dunnington brothers

Donald F. Kern, D.D.S.

Richard D. Dunnington

Wilfred W. "Billy" O'Dell III

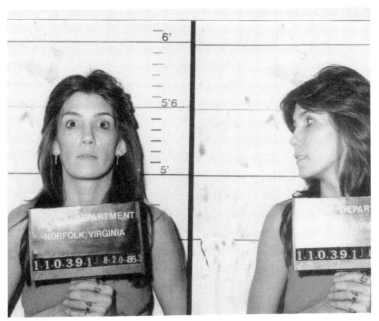

Vicky Wheeless ("Frankie")

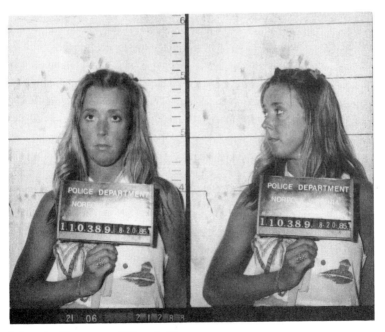

Margo Cassano ("Jamie")

Raymond L. Parsons, Jr.
(deceased)

Alex S. Hargroves, III

Eugene T. Schmidt

Chuck Robb and Bruce Thompson

dward G. Garcia, Jr.

FEDERAL ELECTION COMMISSION
WASHINGTON, D.C. 20463

October 29, 1990

William R. O'Brien, Esq.
Hudgins, Ege and O'Brien
3720 Virginia Beach Boulevard
 Suite 208
Virginia Beach, VA 23452

RE: MUR 2673
     Billy Franklin

Dear Mr. O'Brien:

On October 12, 1990, you were notified that the Federal
Election Commission received an amendment to a complaint from
David McCloud alleging violations of certain sections of the
Federal Election Campaign Act of 1971, as amended, by your
client, Billy Franklin. At that time you were given a copy of
the amendment and informed that a response to the amendment
should be submitted within 15 days of receipt of the
notification.

On October 16, 1990, the Commission received additional
information from the complainant pertaining to the allegations
in the complaint. Enclosed is a copy of this additional
information. As this new information is considered an amendment
to the original complaint, you are hereby afforded an additional
15 days in which to respond to the allegations.

It appears that our October 12, 1990 letter may have caused
some confusion regarding the Act's confidentiality provisions.
As discussed in our prior notification letters, this enforcement
matter will remain confidential in accordance with 2 U.S.C.
§ 437g(a)(4)(b) and § 437g(a)(12)(A) unless the respondents
notify the Commission in writing that they wish the matter to be
made public. No public disclosures regarding any complaint
filed with the Commission, any notification sent by the
Commission, any investigation conducted by the Commission, or
any findings made by the Commission should occur absent the
Commission's receipt of such a waiver from the person(s)
receiving the notification or with respect to whom the action is
taken. 2 U.S.C. § 437g(a)(12)(A); 11 C.F.R. § 111.21(b). When
the Commission receives a waiver of confidentiality, receipt of
the waiver will be acknowledged in writing.

Even when a written waiver of confidentiality pursuant to
2 U.S.C. § 437g(a)(12)(A) has been received and acknowledged by

William R. O'Brien, Esq.
Page 2

the Commission, information regarding respondents who have not
waived confidentiality, if any, remains confidential and you may
not disclose such information until you have been notified by
the Commission that the entire file in this matter has been
closed.   Furthermore, except as provided in 2 U.S.C.
§ 437g(a)(4)(B)(ii) and 11 C.F.R. § 111.20, no information
regarding conciliation efforts may be made public without the
written consent of the respondent and the Commission.   2 U.S.C.
§ 437g(a)(4)(B)(i); 11 C.F.R. § 111.21(b).

     Should you have any questions regarding confidentiality or
any other aspect of this matter, please contact Tony Buckley,
the attorney assigned to this matter, at (202) 376-5690.

                              Sincerely,

                              Lawrence M. Noble
                              General Counsel

                    BY: Lois G. Lerner
                          Associate General Counsel

Enclosure

FEDERAL ELECTION COMMISSION
WASHINGTON, D.C. 20463

August 22, 1988

Mr. William Franklin
Franklin Security Systems
7909 Brookfield Road
Norfolk, VA 23518

RE: MUR 2673
William Franklin

Dear Mr. Franklin:

The Federal Election Commission received a complaint which alleges that you may have violated the Federal Election Campaign Act of 1971, as amended (the "Act"). A copy of the complaint is enclosed. We have numbered this matter MUR 2673. Please refer to this number in all future correspondence.

Under the Act, you have the opportunity to demonstrate in writing that no action should be taken against you in this matter. Please submit any factual or legal materials which you believe are relevant to the Commission's analysis of this matter. Where appropriate, statements should be submitted under oath. Your response, which should be addressed to the General Counsel's Office, must be submitted within 15 days of receipt of this letter. If no response is received within 15 days, the Commission may take further action based on the available information.

This matter will remain confidential in accordance with Section 437g(a)(4)(B) and Section 437g(a)(12)(A) of Title 2 unless you notify the Commission in writing that you wish the matter to be made public. If you intend to be represented by counsel in this matter, please advise the Commission by completing the enclosed form stating the name, address, and telephone number of such counsel, and authorizing such counsel to receive any notifications and other communications from the Commission.

BEFORE THE FEDERAL ELECTIONS COMMISSION

ROBB FOR SENATE,
    Complainant,

v.

JOHN DOE, Employer
  of Mr. William Franklin,
    Respondent

_____

COMPLAINT

1. This complaint is filed on behalf of the Robb for Senate
campaign (FEC I.D. No. COO-221242).

Background

2. More than eighteen months ago, the Republican Party in
Virginia began spreading rumors about former Virginia Governor
Charles S. Robb's association with certain individuals in the
Virginia Beach, Virginia area.

3. In the course of this rumor campaign, both Donald
Huffman, chairman of the Republican Party in Virginia, and
Michael Salster, press secretary for both the Republican Party in
Virginia and Maurice Dawkins' campaign for the Senate, made calls
to the press and to prominent members of the business and civic
communities throughout the state of Virginia attempting to
implicate the former governor in an ongoing investigation
conducted by the U.S. Attorney for the Eastern District of
Virginia into drug use and drug trafficking in the Virginia Beach
area.

4. On May 12, 1988, Ray Garland, a former Republican state
senator from Virginia, published a column in the Roanoke Times
and World News, a Landmark publication, referring to a story
about former Governor Robb on which the Norfolk Virginian-Pilot
was alleged "to be sitting," and which Garland said he had heard
about "from a respectable source." (A copy of the story is
attached)

5. Rose Ellen O'Connor, a reporter from the Norfolk
Virginian Pilot, a Landmark paper, received calls from prominent
Republicans and has spent the past eighteen months trying to
write a story based on those rumors.

W. R. "Buster" O'Brien (left), discussing legal issues with Billy Franklin

Billy Franklin with (left to right) Cindy Upson, office manager at Franklin Security systems, and Diane Heany, investigative supervisor

pens, files and mementos, a glass globe encloses a scorpion suspended in water. Scuttling across the ground, dangerous to the point of death, seeking shade from the unmerciful heat and, also, seeking prey.

Franklin smiled, nodded to the scorpion and left the room. He had an investigation to work on.

Chapter Seventeen

Federal Power

"Robb complains about private investigator"
Headline in The Virginian-Pilot
and The Ledger-Star,
September 15, 1988

On August 24, 1988, within days of his call from Melton, Bill Franklin received his copy of the Federal Election Commission complaint. Dated August 22, it arrived at the offices of Franklin Security Systems by certified mail. The reference number was MUR 2673.

The complaint, filed by the Robb for Senate campaign, listed six background items and seven items pertaining to the alleged violation itself.

The background statements were a laundry list of loosely related circumstances, none of which had anything to do with Bill Franklin:

—that the Republican Party in Virginia had been the source of the rumors concerning former Governor Robb's association with "certain individuals" in the Virginia Beach area;

—that Donald Huffman, chairman of the Republican Party in Virginia, and Michael Salster, press secretary for the Republican Party in Virginia and Maurice Dawkins' campaign for the Senate, made calls to the press and to prominent individuals trying to implicate Robb in the drug investigation;

—that a newspaper columnist in Roanoke had written a story saying that the Norfolk newspapers were "sitting on" a story about Robb; that reporter Rose Ellen O'-Connor had spent eighteen months "trying to write a story" based on the rumors;

—that Alicia Mundy, a reporter for *Regardie's* magazine, said she had received calls from prominent Republicans alleging Robb's involvement with drugs;

—and that the U.S. Attorney for the Eastern District of Virginia had stated that Governor Robb was never a subject of his office's investigation and that there was no evidence to connect Robb with drug use or sales or "even attendance at parties where drugs might have been in use."

The seven items pertaining to the alleged violation by Franklin set forth these facts:

—that Franklin had been conducting inquiries into Robb's activities;

—that Franklin had interviewed Virginia Beach residents, including Jean [sic] Schmidt;

—that Franklin had told individuals he had received "a handsome retainer" for his work;

—that the Robb for Senate campaign did not believe that Franklin's activities were on behalf of a media organization;

—that Franklin's activities appeared to be directly related to the Senate campaign and that his retainer and expenses should be reported as either an independent expenditure or a campaign expenditure and/or in-kind contribution;

—that no quarterly report filed with the FEC contained a report of the costs of Franklin's service;and that no individual or group had reported Franklin's expenses as an independent expenditure.

In the conclusion of the complaint, the Robb for Senate campaign requested that the FEC find probable cause to believe that Franklin's employer, or the recipient of an in-kind contribution from Franklin's employer, had violated the Federal Election Campaign Act and the regulations of the Commission.

The complaint was signed by David K. McCloud, Chairman, Robb for Senate.

"What the hell is this?" Bill Franklin shouted to the air around him.

He picked up the phone to call his friend Buster O'Brien. Chuck Robb had just tweaked the scorpion.

Four days later, on Sunday, August 28, Rose Ellen O'Connor's story was splashed across the top of the front page of *The Virginian-Pilot and The Ledger-Star*:

"ROBB ENJOYED GLITZY VA. BEACH SOCIAL SCENE"

Chapter Eighteen

Robb on the Run

"I've said repeatedly, and I've told any number of reporters over the years, that I do like to enjoy my privacy and in my strictly personal time I like to have a good time. . . I'm not a cardboard figure."
Senator Charles Robb, *The Virginian-Pilot* and
The Ledger-Star, August 28, 1988

The focus of the newspaper story was Robb's close association with ten of the men who had been drawn into the federal cocaine probe. It placed Robb at parties where the drug was used, but also acknowledged that "More than 200 interviews conducted by *The Virginian-Pilot and The Ledger-Star.* . .produced no evidence that Robb used cocaine."

O'Connor didn't have an eyewitness either.

The interview that Rose Ellen O'Connor had with Robb prior to publication of her article resulted from extensive negotiations between his attorney and campaign director and *The Virginian-Pilot and The Ledger-Star.*

At first, Robb agreed to the interview, then changed his mind and said no. Next he said he would do an interview for the newspaper, but not with O'Connor. After that, he said he would do the interview with O'Connor but only if the newspaper agreed to withhold publication of the story until after the Democratic nominating convention in June, a condition to which the newspaper would not agree.

In the end, O'Connor did the interview with Robb at his Richmond office in the presence of James Raper, the newspaper's managing editor; Dale Eiseman, the newspaper's state editor; and David McCloud, Robb's administrative assistant.

Robb stated, as he had when the rumors first surfaced, "I have never, ever seen or been involved in any way, shape or form with drugs."

He suggested that the drug probe, which was headed by Attorney Henry E. Hudson, a Republican, was politically tainted and that some state Republicans tried to use the investigation to "smear" him.

In a written statement, Hudson said that he had assured members of both political parties that Robb was not under investigation.

"A prosecutor's charge," he wrote, "is to pursue all leads in a criminal investigation firmly and fairly. Unfortunately, those responsible for such investigations cannot maintain uniform popularity in all quarters."

Robb also blamed the newspapers for keeping the story alive by continuing to conduct interviews with people in the resort area.

He described Virginia Beach as his place for "letting off a little steam."

The newspaper outlined the relationship between Robb and ten of the people who had been involved in the drug investigation: Bruce Thompson; Ricky and Bobby Dunnington;, John Aspinwall, a party regular and part-owner of a chain of storage facilities; Donald Kern; Billy O'Dell; Alex Hargroves, owner of Old Dominion Engineering, Inc., who said he had purchased drugs from his employee, the late Ray Parsons; Gene Schmidt, and John Bennis. The newspaper quoted Thompson as saying in an interview that he denied any involvement with illegal activity and that he was always mindful of his position as a close friend and political appointee of the former governor and would never have engaged in activities that might compromise Robb.

Robb, in return, said that Thompson had gotten "a bad rap from a couple of folks" because while achieving financial success, he "stepped on a few toes."

Robb confirmed that he had been to two parties at John Bennis' home, but expressed surprise that Bennis was linked to cocaine. He said he never saw the drug.

Robb confirmed that he had been at the Fourth of July party at Ray Parsons' house. He said he saw no evidence of drugs. Robb said that he had christened yachts — both named "Sea Raven" — for the Dunnington brothers but that he did not know them well.

Robb said that he did not recall Donald Kern at all. In addition, Robb said that he had terminated his relationship with Ricky Haycox after learning in 1983 that Haycox had been convicted in 1981 of highway bid-rigging. Robb said that he had subsequently seen Haycox only rarely.

The newspaper reported, however, that others close to Haycox, including his estranged wife, said the two men socialized frequently as late as the summer of 1986 on Haycox's boat.

In talking about his relationship with Eddie Garcia, Robb acknowledged that he had cut his ties to the Virginia Beach businessman during the early 1980's after receiving what he called "apparently. . .some erroneous information."

Robb said that he and Garcia had patched up their differences early in 1988 and that Garcia had made a contribution to his current Senate campaign.

O'Connor recalled later that during the course of their interview, Robb seemed nervous and became angry with her at one point, standing up from his chair, and saying that he wouldn't answer any questions. A few moments later he returned to his seat and continued to talk with her.

Another player in Robb's life was introduced to the public on that Sunday morning: Tai Collins' photo appeared, along with statements from her that she had attended parties with Robb and some of the men implicated in the drug probe. Collins, who said she was 20 when she first met and dated Robb, told O'Connor that she "sometimes found Robb's associations puzzling."

"I always wondered how he got to be friends with some of those people," Collins said.

Bill Franklin noticed that any reference to other women in Robb's life, or within the milieu of the

Oceanfront parties that were reported, was absent. Franklin's observations were concurrent with many others in the journalistic, political and law enforcement arenas who felt *The Virginian-Pilot* story appeared not merely restrained but indirect and watered down in its reporting of Robb's activities. Franklin learned later that the newspaper editors imposed a specific policy which absolutely prohibited the reporter's use of unnamed sources in the Robb story.

Two years after doing the story, O'Connor, who went on to work for The Los Angeles *Times*, said that although she had discovered clear links between Robb associates and prostitutes she was never able to confirm his activities. A number of hookers, she said, had confirmed having sex for money with Bruce Thompson and being paid by Thompson to appear at parties where Robb would also be present.

None of them, however, would go on the record as saying that they had sex with Governor Robb.

The newspaper, she added, was only interested in printing a story that was absolutely solid. "We wanted to do something almost scholarly, not sensationalism," she said.

O'Connor said that she had no real understanding of the effect cocaine had on people until she worked this story.

"It was so depressing," she recalled. As an example, she said, "Ray Parsons was a shell of a person. Pathetic. Not even human. He reminded me of a lizard."

She had qualms at the beginning of her work on the Robb story, she said, about "digging into someone's personal life. But once I saw the pattern of who he was hanging around with, I got over it."

Bill Franklin read the newspaper coverage with intense interest. He knew that it would start the Oceanfront hive buzzing all over again, bring him more information.

But first there was the FEC to deal with.

Chapter Nineteen

An Education in FEC

"The respondent believes that this complaint was filed and then leaked to the news media by the Robb for Senate campaign in an obvious attempt to manipulate the FEC for political gain."
Bill Franklin to the FEC, September 1988

$\mathbf{F}$ranklin quickly realized that he had been right: no one around town knew much about federal election laws or the commission that oversees them. O'Brien was able to locate a 1985 copy of the Federal Election Campaign Laws. With some advice and help from O'Brien, Franklin drafted his answer to the FEC. The Federal Election Commission was established in 1971 to oversee campaign contributions. The Commission is composed of the Secretary of the Senate and the Clerk of the House of Representatives, ex officio and without the right to vote, and six members appointed by the president by and with the consent of the Senate. No more than three members may belong to the same political party. The members of the Commission serve rotating six-year terms.

They meet monthly, or at the call of any member.

In addition, the Commission appoints a staff director and a general counsel, both of whom are paid employees of the Commission.

The powers given to the Federal Election Commission in order to regulate campaign expenditures were far-reaching, and — as Bill Franklin was about to find out — could be expanded judicially to suit the Commission's purposes. In their quest to keep tabs on money donated to, or spent on behalf of, candidates for federal office, they have exclusive jurisdiction over civil enforcement of all the policies that fall under their purview. Although confidentiality is guaranteed in an FEC proceeding, Franklin chose to request in the first paragraph of his cover letter that the matter be made public.

In the second paragraph he told the FEC that he believed no reply was even necessary on his part since he was not named as the respondent in the action, but rather that "John Doe" was. Nonetheless, he said, "with an abundance of caution," he would attempt to answer the complaint.

In addition to answering the points of the complaint, Franklin said he had no knowledge of telephone calls made by anyone, that he was unaware of statements made by the United States attorney, and that he had never met anyone directly associated with the campaign. He admitted that he was conducting inquiries related to Robb's activities; he admitted that he had talked with Gene Schmidt and other residents of Virginia Beach. When it came to the identity of the person who had hired him, he invoked the attorney/client privilege and refused to tell.

After answering each of the complaints, Franklin added a section of additional comments, citing the Robb for Senate Committee's long-standing knowledge of the rumors, and the fact that he had interviewed people of varying political persuasions, Republicans and Democrats alike.

In his comment 17, he wrote:

"That the respondent believes that this complaint was filed and then leaked to the news media by the Robb for Senate campaign in an obvious attempt to manipulate the FEC for political gain. The timing of the filing of this complaint and subsequent newspaper leak make it obvious that the Robb Campaign is attempting to diffuse a story in *The Virginian-Pilot* and *The Ledger-Star* regarding some of his aforementioned activities."

In comment 18, the scorpion began to stir:

"That the respondent has had threats made on his life if he continues this investigation. One of the threats is on tape, and a police report has been filed with Lt. Frank Drew of the Virginia Beach Police Department. Further, the respondent believes this present complaint is merely another attempt to intimidate the respondent into terminating his inquiry."

Comment 19 went for the sting:

"That the respondent is not a named defendant in this complaint and that there are no allegations of wrongdoing by the respondent which is further evidence of the fact that this complaint is politically motivated."

At the end, he asked for the complaint to be dismissed. He mailed his answer to the FEC on September 7.

Two days later he received the second salvo from the FEC. It had been written the day before his answer was mailed.

Chapter Twenty

Once Was Not Enough: Addendum

*"Robb is incensed by Billy Franklin's whole invol-
vement in this," (State Sen. Moody E. "Sonny")
Stallings said.*

The Virginian-Pilot and The Ledger-Star,
September 15, 1988

Dated September 6, 1988, the Addendum to the
original complaint went even further in its allegations.

First, it said that Franklin had previously done investigative work for Joe Canada, Jr. in connection with the
political campaign against Charles Robb.

Second, it stated that state Senator Moody E. Stallings,
Jr. had received a telephone call from a source within the
law firm of W.R. O'Brien and that this individual had
heard Franklin claim, during a visit to the law firm, that
he possessed signed affidavits from two people who alleged they had witnessed Robb using illegal drugs. Stallings, they said, further reported that Franklin and O'Brien
were close friends.

The third background statement was this:

"The affidavits described by Mr. Franklin, if they exist,
are categorically and unequivocally false."

The final statement reiterated the complaint that
Franklin's fee did not appear on any FEC report.

Bill Franklin was enraged. He fired off his answer later
that week, saying to the first claim that he had no
knowledge of that claim, and to the second that he denied
the claim. As for the existence of the affidavits, he neither
confirmed nor denied, and as to the final statement that
he had "no knowledge of any reason why any report
should be filed with the FEC."

Franklin wasn't going to let it go at just answering the complaint, of course. He added seven more additional comments of his own.

Yes, Franklin wrote, he had done work for a lot of people regardless of their political affiliations during the course of his career.

He had not, Franklin pointed out, visited the law offices of Mr. O'Brien for more than two years, even though they were close personal friends.

"The respondent," he wrote, "also maintains a close friendship with several other lawyers whose political affiliations are Democratic, Republican and Independent. In the City of Virginia Beach, politicians and would-be politicians change political affiliations more often than their underwear." And Franklin reaffirmed that he invoked the client/attorney privilege in regard to the name of his client.

Franklin also reminded the Federal Election Commission that he was not a named defendant in the complaint and repeated that there were no allegations of wrongdoing by him, ". . .which," he wrote, "is further evidence of the fact that this complaint is politically motivated."

On Friday, September 9, two days after he received the FEC's additional allegations, Bill Franklin arrived home exhausted and put his feet up. Maybe, he thought, he could get some rest this weekend.

But before Franklin could relax, the telephone rang. It was his old friend, Jimmy Darden. Darden said he needed Franklin to come over to his house right away. Someone was there who needed to speak to him.

Bill Franklin put his shoes back on and left the house.

Chapter Twenty-one

If We Can't Scare You, Maybe We Can Bribe You

"A great deal of money has already been invested in Chuck Robb, and will continue to be invested in order to pave the way for Robb to become a presidential candidate."

David Johnson, An emissary
September 1988

Jimmy Darden and Bill Franklin were hunting and fishing buddies. They'd shared more than one bottle of brandy trying to thaw out after freezing in duck blinds in Back Bay. When Darden called that Friday night, he said that an acquaintance of his wanted to talk to Franklin about the Robb case, right then. All Bill Franklin wanted to do was rest.

But friendships, especially long-standing ones, are important to Bill Franklin. When the people who have known him for ten, twenty, thirty years — men like Charlie Irwin and Norman Bell, who coached Bill when he became a 32nd degree Mason — sit around and talk about him, they often mention his loyalty to his friends.

When one of the men in their closely knit group was grief-stricken over his divorce, he became suicidal. One night, the man began drinking heavily and then made some phone calls, saying that he was armed and was going to shoot himself. Friends gathered outside the man's darkened house, panicked and bewildered. Someone called Bill Franklin.

He was there, they said, in the blink of an eye. He assessed the situation quickly and then told the others to just wait there. He entered the dark house where an armed man waited, despondent.

Bill Franklin even admits to having been a little afraid as he made his way down the hallway to the bedroom. But, he adds as an afterthought, someone had to do something. The man in there was a friend. And you don't abandon friends.

It took a long time, an hour or so. The two old friends talked. The man finally gave Franklin his gun. The two men emerged from the house together.

So there was no question that when Jimmy Darden called, Bill Franklin would go. He put his gun on and left the house.

The man he met at Jimmy Darden's house was David Johnson, who introduced himself as a business associate of several local prominent businessmen. The three men sat in Darden's living room.

Johnson said that he had been asked by a member of Hunton and Williams, Robb's law firm, to talk with Franklin about who had hired him.

"A great deal of money has already been invested in Chuck Robb," Johnson explained, "and will continue to be invested in order to pave the way for Robb to become a presidential candidate."

He and others, Johnson said, were of the personal opinion that Robb was "stupid as hell," but that with the right guidance he could do good things for Virginia as well as for other special interest groups.

Franklin listened with interest and no small amount of disdain.

"And how would these people feel," he asked at last, "if it turned out that Robb had actually been snorting cocaine?"

Johnson was not moved. It didn't really matter, he said; the backers didn't care. "The money interests in Chuck Robb come a lot higher than the people of Virginia," he said.

Franklin was stunned at Johnson's attitude.

As Johnson continued to talk, the proposition became clear. Franklin could be in the unique position of being able to continue his investigation and make additional money if he gave his information on Robb to Johnson. Although no dollar amounts were offered, a new custom-built sportfishing boat came into the discussion. And Franklin knew that the price on a new Buddy Davis boat was over $400,000.

Throughout the conversation, Jimmy Darden looked ill, as if, Franklin recalled, "he wished that he had been somewhere else. "The men parted with nothing resolved. Franklin had provided no information about his client or the investigation. They would, they agreed, meet at some later date.

Franklin had no intention of meeting with David Johnson again in his life.

But now he knew how worried the Robb camp really was. Tom Smith, a former business partner of David Johnson and also a long-time friend of Franklin's, later confirmed for him that Johnson had first approached Smith to be the go-between to Franklin.

According to Smith, Johnson had indicated that an attorney from Robb's Richmond law firm was interested in talking to Franklin to see if they could determine who Franklin's client was and what information he already had.

"Did he give you any indication that they would be offering anything to me?" Franklin asked.

"That was my impression," Smith said. "My response after I thought about it. . .I said something to the effect. . .well, I don't think Mr. Franklin will be receptive."

Smith also said that he pressed Johnson to give him a figure as to how much money would be offered to Franklin for the information.

Johnson said he would get back to him with a firm figure to offer Franklin. When Smith next saw Johnson about ten days later, Johnson said that another liaison had been found and that the meeting with Franklin had already taken place.

In early October, 1988, Franklin finally located Gennie Zollos, a former girlfriend of Billy O'Dell. She had been at the Tarzan and Jane contest at Jungle Falls and at the party afterwards at Thompson and Schmidt's house.

Thompson, she said, had fixed Robb up with K.K., the winner of the contest.

The scene at the party had been wild, she said, with cocaine lines laid out in the bathroom and the bedroom. Although she hadn't seen him do so in her presence, she said, she felt sure that Robb had not only been aware of the cocaine but had been snorting it as well. He acted, she said, "weird."

During the evening, she and Billy O'Dell had gone for a walk on the beach with Robb and K.K. The couples parted when Robb announced that he and K.K. were going to go skinny dipping. It took only a few weeks for Franklin to find K.K. She was, at first, amenable to meeting with him. The day before they were to meet, however, she called him back.

"I have nothing to say to you," she said flatly.

Maybe the timing was coincidence; maybe not. That fall, the Army Corps of Engineers, a federal agency, brought a claim against Bill and Keetie, charging that the pier behind their house, built 12 years previously, had not been constructed in accordance with the exact dimensions submitted by the contractor. The Franklins' time and money began to go toward fighting yet another federal action.

At the same time, Chuck Robb was dodging new charges of his own.

Chapter Twenty-two

Seagull Redux

"Robb associated with a number of wealthy businessmen and others who later were caught up in a federal investigation into drug use in Tidewater, but has insisted only that he was 'naive' about some of his social companions."

The Washington Times, October 8, 1988

On Friday, October 7, 1988, The Washington *Times* broke a story under the headline:

ROBB'S BUSY SOCIAL LIFE LIMITED CRIME PROBE, AGENTS SAY

The article stated that state and local undercover agents in Virginia Beach were ordered by their superiors not to mention Robb's repeated appearances with key figures in an investigation of illegal gambling and organized crime ties to area businessmen when he was governor of Virginia.

The investigation was Operation Seagull. The story The Washington *Times* was running was the same one that reporter John Sherwood had been blocked from pursuing for *The Virginian-Pilot and The Ledger-Star* three years earlier.

Reporter George Archibald wrote that Robb was told of the investigation in 1982 by Gerald Baliles, who was then the state attorney general and who later became governor. Robb was seen with targets of the probe for at least two years afterwards, often at social functions at which cocaine was openly used and prostitutes were occasionally present.

"His appearances from 1982 to 1984 at events under surveillance by investigators were so frequent that the order to exclude him from the probe seriously hampered it, according to state and local agents involved in the undercover operation," Archibald reported.

One undercover police officer who asked not be named in the article said, "We were ordered not to include his name in our reports or [the references] would be taken out."

The article further said that surveillances often had to be shut down when Robb appeared, which led to the entire probe being ended.

The undercover agent quoted in the story was still involved in police undercover work and said that he could not be named because it would jeopardize law enforcement operation and open him to retaliation.

His account was confirmed to The Washington *Times'* reporter by a police supervisor involved in undercover operations at the state and local level who also asked not to be named.

Robb's response to the report was to refuse repeated requests for an interview through campaign staff officials and his personal attorney, Robert Nusbaum of Norfolk. In a prepared statement released through his campaign spokeswoman, Julia Sutherland, Robb stated that he had "absolutely no knowledge" of a state police cover-up of his private associations and activities while governor.

The newspaper story detailed Robb's association with Eddie Garcia, who was a prime target of the undercover probe. On one occasion in 1982, Garcia asked undercover agent Louis Slade, whom Garcia believed to be the high-rolling, wheeler-dealer "Larry Watson," to fly Robb from Richmond to Virginia Beach on "Watson's" private seven-seat plane.

The conversation between Garcia and "Watson" was taped by the undercover agent.

Agents immediately reported Garcia's request to transport the governor to Robert Berryman, who was then deputy director of the state police criminal investigations bureau in Richmond. Berryman notified Jay Cochran, the bureau director who had been appointed by Robb.

An undercover agent told the *Times*: "The [stuff] hit the fan. They told us not to fly Robb."

Berryman, who was director of state police criminal investigations in 1988 when the story was printed, said he didn't recall the incident.

Jay Cochran, who had gone to work in Pennsylvania after Operation Seagull and then returned to Virginia where he was appointed by Baliles to head the investigative branch of the state liquor board, said he had no comments to make in confirmation or denial of the story.

David McCloud, chairman of the Robb for Senate campaign, stated in the article that then Attorney General Baliles had, in fact, warned Robb of the undercover operation rather than allow him to become a party to it.

"The governor was advised through official channels that there was an undercover investigation and that there was a plane which had been arranged to take him to Virginia Beach for purposes of attending a function," McCloud said.

"That official source was the attorney general of Virginia," he added.

"He was told that because of the investigation, he should not — he should just be aware of that and he should stay away from it," McCloud said. "And he did do that. He did not go on the plane."

The story went on to point out that while Operation Seagull and other joint state and local undercover probes were being conducted from 1982 to 1984, Robb was frequently observed by police socializing with surveillance targets at private events and parties, according to police sources, even after Baliles' 1982 warning not to take the plane flight or to be associated with Garcia.

The article went on to explain how Bruce Thompson had become a target of Operation Seagull in 1979 and ensuing criminal probes because he had once worked for Anthony "Tony G" Gargulio, an associate of the Gambino organized crime family.

During the following week, the allegations of a cover-up on Robb's behalf became a front-page political football. Robert J. Humphreys, formerly Deputy Commonwealth's Attorney and now Commonwealth's Attorney of Virginia Beach, was quoted as saying that the case against organized gambling had been "damaged by the cover-up" and that the state police shut down the investigation when Robb showed up, hindering prosecutions.

A day after his remarks were made public in The Washington *Times*, Humphreys told *The Virginian-Pilot*: "Those words never came out of my mouth."

The Virginian-Pilot once again criticized the continuing revelations about a state police cover-up. In an editorial dated October 13, 1988, and based on Mr. Humphreys' denial, they wrote: "Based on what has been revealed, the General Assembly does not have evidence that would justify convening an inquiry. Unless some substantial evidence turns up, the matter ought to be dropped — political campaign or not."

What the newspaper editors failed to tell its readers was that Mr. Humphreys' conversations with The Washington *Times* reporter were reproduced quote for quote in the October 12 edition of The Washington *Times*.

It was clear to the *Times'* readers that Humphreys' quotes had not been manufactured as he had charged in *The Virginian-Pilot*.

However, *The Virginian-Pilot's* audience was not afforded the same luxury of judgement. In the midst of the newspaper coverage of the alleged cover-ups and calls from Republicans for an investigation and inquiry into the state police, the Robb for Senate campaign returned a $4,000 campaign contribution from Eddie Garcia, who had just been indicted on a felony gambling conspiracy charge in Dinwiddie County.

A week after the cover-up story broke, Virginia state police officials refused to allow officers who had served as undercover investigators and the governor's protective detail to be interviewed by the press.

In the meantime, the House of Delegates' Militia and Police Committee voted unanimously to delay a decision on possibly investigating the cover-up allegations until after the November 8 elections.

Robb won the senatorial election in an overwhelming defeat of Republican Maurice Dawkins, a relatively unknown black Baptist minister who, according to polls conducted throughout the campaign, had never garnered more than 17 percent of the vote. No investigation of the cover-up allegations has ever been undertaken. And, as many people have told Franklin, none ever will be.

Chapter Twenty-three

Tough Times

"Am I tough enough?"
from a song of the same name
The Fabulous Thunderbirds

By the time the senatorial election finally rolled around in November of 1988, Bill and Keetie Franklin felt as if they were dodging shots from all directions.

On October 28, the Federal Election Commission ordered Franklin to reveal the name of his client and to disclose any information that had been given to the client and or anyone else concerning Robb's private life.

The Washington *Times* quoted Franklin's defiant response: "I'm not telling them anything."

After he received the order from the FEC, Franklin realized that he must either comply or prepare for a lengthy court action. To do that, he would need experienced legal counsel.

Inquiries turned up the name of a Washington, D.C. law firm that specialized in Federal Election Commission matters. When Franklin called, a member of the firm told him that he would be required to provide a $10,000 retainer in advance and that he should be prepared to spend a minimum of $50,000. And that figure did not include any Federal Court action.

The firm's course of action, the attorney said, would be to first negotiate with Robb's people directly.

"Hell," Franklin thought, "I can do that myself for free and make a hell of a lot of money if I'm willing to compromise my client."

Through a series of meetings during the following week, Bill Franklin met with his client, Dr. Williams, and attorney Buster O'Brien. An agreement was reached:

Williams would pay for O'Brien to defend Franklin, a fee far more reasonable than the one quoted by the Washington, D.C. law firm.

Franklin and O'Brien prepared to face down the FEC.

"What else," Franklin wondered, "can possibly happen?"

The notification that he would be audited by the Internal Revenue Service came in the middle of November. High Seas Sportfishing, Inc., their charter boat business, was under scrutiny. The audit took eight hours; Keetie's meticulous records saved the day.

Bill Franklin and everyone around him were being ground into fine powder. As he looked back over 1988, he was astounded at what he had already been through, how tangled it had all become, how the bedrock foundation of his life was shifting and changing under his feet.

He thought about the offer of the new boat. He thought about getting these damned federal people off his back. He remembered with a sense of deep melancholy how sweet his life had been before.

And what did he have, really? A lot of people saying they had heard, or they had believed, or after-the-fact told him they had seen. But nothing to hang his hat on. Nothing to confirm, once and for all, that Chuck Robb had used cocaine and had sex with women at the parties.

Franklin's payments from Dr. Williams had stopped months before. What he had expected to be a fairly quick assessment of truth and lies had turned into a far longer and deeper investigation than either of them had ever anticipated. After the initial retainer payment of $2,500 in the spring, Dr. Williams had paid an additional $10,000 in several payments, all in response to Franklin's telephone calls that he would need additional money to continue the investigation.

The physician, stunned at the turn of events, the death threats, and the FEC suit, had indicated he could not afford to pay Franklin any more money.

Nonetheless, Franklin chose to continue the investigation. It had his name on it now; he was in it all the way.

To stop would be a capitulation he could not live with. He knew that he would have to take it upon himself to finance the remainder of the investigation.

It had become, after all, a matter of principle.

"And how much worse could it get?" he wondered. If the Robb supporters were so serious about what he already knew that they would offer him a new boat worth several hundred thousand dollars, what were they willing to do to him if he refused to quit? And what would they do if he found out even more?

Late at night that November, Bill Franklin sat in the dark in the big living room, alone, staring out at the water.

Surrounded by antiques, keepsakes, figurines and photos accumulated during their lifetime together, he feared for what would happen to Keetie if anything happened to him.

The big game fish, which he had landed so triumphantly, arched on the walls above him. There had been a time when he thought that the lure of those big fish was the ultimate challenge, that trolling the sea in anticipation of the strike and the final fight that crippled fingers and cramped arms for hours afterward, was as fine a sense of accomplishment as any man could expect to feel.

He thought back over what the months had brought to him. Lots of trouble. Little satisfaction. No completion. No strike. No win.

Not yet, anyway. So far, his investigation had been like all those hours when he would search the water's shimmer for a sign of the catch that eluded him: like the marlin, like the swordfish, like all the big fish that had tried to elude him, Bill Franklin knew that the truth about Robb was out there, under there. Big fish dive deep. And if you want to win you just go deeper with them.

When Bill Franklin thought about winning he thought about Vince Lombardi.

"Winning," Lombardi once said, "is a habit. There is no room for second place. An army, a political party, a business. The principles are the same. The object is to win, to beat the other guy."

And then J.C. Russell came to his mind. J.C. was another old friend, and in his mind Franklin heard J.C. Russell talking to him, saying:

"Tough times don't last, but tough people do."

That, Bill Franklin knew, was the question he was asking himself.

Was he tough enough?

He grappled with the question as the winter came on, wet and cold. The holidays were coming, but it was difficult to be excited. They were short of money, short of work, short of time and long on stress.

They made it through Christmas.

Right after that, Bill Franklin's mother got sick.

Chapter Twenty-four

Crucible and Decision

*"Billy, never go looking for a fight. But if you can't
avoid it, don't give one damn inch."*
Veva Franklin, Bill Franklin's mother

On Sunday, January 29, 1989, Bill Franklin was on
the road just outside of Atlanta, Georgia, when Keetie
tracked him down. He'd set out with sales materials to
present to other security companies throughout the
South and West in the hope of signing them up as
subcontractors for the psychological honesty test that
Franklin had successfully adopted.

His mother's cancer had been a reality since the fall,
but her radiation and chemotherapy treatments seemed
to be keeping it at bay. When he spoke to her on New
Year's Day, 1989, she was in fine spirits and said she was
feeling well.

On Sunday, January 29, she had a stroke. The message
came from California: come at once.

His first instinct was to fly, to hop the first plane to the
Coast. And then he remembered the boxes in the back of
the car. As always, he had the entire files of the Robb
investigation with him. There was no way he could risk
leaving the car in an airport parking lot.

He canceled his appointments and headed the Porsche
west. Bill Franklin hadn't seen his mother in three years.
When his brother Bob picked him up at the motel, he
tried to prepare Bill for her condition.

Nothing could have prepared him sufficiently for the
shock he felt when he walked into that hospital room. The
robust, hardy, hard-nosed woman who had raised him was
virtually skin and bones, totally helpless, with tubes in her
arm and an oxygen mask over her mouth and nose. When

she saw him coming toward her, she tried to raise herself off the pillows.

Bill Franklin broke down sobbing.

At the end of the most excruciating week of his life, Bill Franklin's mother was dead, buried, and he was speeding eastward through the Texas night toward Virginia. He was exhausted, nearly blind with sorrow, and felt the weight of the Robb investigation settling over him once again.

He thought about what he believed about life; and he thought about his mother and all that she had taught him.

It seemed as if he heard her talking to him as he drove across the roads of his childhood.

"Billy," she'd said when he was very, very young, "never go looking for a fight. But if you can't avoid it, don't give one damn inch."

He had never backed down. Not from anything. Growing up in the war-time housing project called Hilltop Circle in Chula Vista, with hundreds of other poor boys from Arkansas and Texas and Oklahoma, he had backed down from nothing. As he grew, he grew big, his massive frame filling out, formidable. A football scholarship — one of 25 he was offered — got him into the University of San Diego; his intelligence and diligence kept him there.

The same attributes had kept him going during his investigation of Chuck Robb. He thought back over that past year and where his investigation had led him.

And then he heard his mother again, just two months earlier, speaking to her grown son just as she had when he was a boy. "Honey," she said, "Don't let them scare you off. Just do what you think is right."

Breathing that familiar clear air, he knew, knew that, really, he had no choice.

It was driving home, then, making his way through the darkness of west Texas, that Bill Franklin knew this: There was nothing they could do to make him stop his investigation. Not a damned thing. He had reached down deep inside, taken a good look, and answered at last the question that had been nagging at him, eating him alive for all these months.

He didn't know the meaning of quitting and he wasn't going to learn it now.

The Porsche leapt as he pushed on the accelerator.

Billy Franklin was going back to Virginia Beach.

Chapter Twenty-five

Being Ground Into Fine Powder

"Am I to understand that anybody who investigates any person who is a candidate for political office must be in a position to hire his counsel to be able to face a star chamber proceeding? Is that what we've come down to?"

The Honorable Robert Doumar, May 1989

When Bill Franklin returned to work on February 13, 1989, his determination was complete. First, the business needed to be brought out of its slump; then, he would get back to Chuck Robb. The harassing telephone calls started almost at once. Night and day, at home, at work. Dozens a day. Unrelenting. And they were always the same: a few moments of dead silence and then the click of a receiver being replaced.

Finally, Franklin contacted the telephone company and a trap was put on his home telephone. After two weeks, the report came back. The calls were being placed from pay phones all over Virginia Beach and the surrounding cities.

Bill and Keetie had never had an unlisted telephone number. If someone wanted — or needed — to reach Bill Franklin they could do so. He liked to be accessible to people who might need him. He knew an unlisted number was an option; he chose not to take it. He was determined not to give anyone that kind of satisfaction.

The trash was the next to go. It's an old investigative trick, but it nonetheless surprised Franklin the first time he noticed that his neighbors' garbage was still beside the road, waiting to be picked up, and his, put out the night before, was gone.

He did two things: he bought paper shredders for his home and his office. And, just for fun, he and his employees started to put little messages into the trash that went out.

Most of what happened wasn't fun at all, though. Franklin's home, office and car phones were checked for taps. The office doors were kept locked and all the employees became conscious of whether or not they were being followed on the road. Franklin's silver Porsche, in particular, is not hard to spot. On at least one occasion, he realized he was being followed and led his pursuer down a dead end street. The other car, containing two men, stopped when the driver realized he was about to be trapped and turned around, speeding away.

In late February, twin blizzards one week apart brought the Hampton Roads area to a standstill. Just after the second one, Franklin received a call from the dockmaster at the marina where the "Top Hook" was tied up. The boat, he said, had been broken into.

The front hatch cover was pried off and the screen was kicked in. Everything not nailed down was stolen and the built-in entertainment center was destroyed. The hatch cover had been left off; a foot of snow covered the exposed V-berth. Repair and replacement cost Franklin $21,000.

The reporters continued to call him now and then, nosing around for any potential story, often offering support and, sometimes, information.

During one of those calls from a reporter in Washington, D.C., Franklin was told that political pressure was being placed on him from both parties, Republicans and Democrats alike. The word was out, the reporter said, that Virginia's Republican Senator John Warner had struck a deal with the Democrats and that, as a result of their agreement, Warner would be able to run unopposed in the next election in 1990.

Robb and Warner's top aides were close, the reporter told Franklin, and certain Republicans were helping to keep the pressure on him. Franklin was dumbfounded.

As the spring of 1989 neared, so did Franklin's confrontation with the Federal Elections Commission.

On March 21, 1989, attorneys for the Federal Election Commission filed a petition with the United States District Court for the Eastern District for an order to show cause and to enforce the administrative order requiring Franklin to name his client and reveal the information in his investigation.

On April 13, Buster O'Brien responded, citing once again Franklin's attorney/client privilege. He took the FEC to task for violating a section of the United States Code when it leaked its original petition to the press before Franklin had even been notified. And he called the FEC's action nothing more than "official curiosity," which is against the law.

During the next six weeks, the two sides duked it out at hearings before the Honorable Robert G. Doumar. They jockeyed for position on issues of jurisdiction, proper service on Bill Franklin as the first "John Doe" case in the history of the FEC, and the powers of the FEC.

On May 25, O'Brien appeared on behalf of Franklin, and Michael Allen Dymersky appeared for the Plaintiff, the Federal Elections Commission, before Judge Doumar.

The original report submitted to the FEC commissioners on October 25, 1988, by FEC General Counsel Lawrence Nobel (at the conclusion of which he advises that they compel Franklin to say who hired him) is an interesting study of a justice maxim stood on its head: A person is assumed guilty until he proves his innocence. The report notes that "the complainant stops short of specifically alleging a link between [Republicans named in the complaint] and Franklin's current investigation will not be considered an independent [campaign] expenditure where the facts uncovered by the investigation are not made public."

Nonetheless, Nobel concluded that "because it is not known at this time who paid Franklin for his services. . .this office recommends that the Commission find reason to believe that unknown person(s) violated [FEC reporting requirements]."

It seemed clear that Judge Doumar had some reservations about helping set a precedent for the FEC to investigate anyone who has a complaint filed against him. At one point during the hearing, he asked FEC lawyer Michael Dymersky, "Am I to understand that anybody who investigates any person who is a candidate for political office must be in a position to hire his counsel to be able to face a star chamber proceeding? Is that what we've come down to?"

After a grilling of Dymersky revealed that the FEC had never questioned any of the Republicans named in the complaint, Doumar said, "I thought the Commission was conducting an investigation. When you go after one person and you don't ask anybody else. . .do you think that's an investigation?"

Franklin says now that he knew it was all over at the very end, when Doumar — who had seemed at times so sympathetic to their side — looked directly at Franklin and said, "I want to make it abundantly clear, there are strong powers given the Federal Election Commission, and the reason for these powers is primarily to keep election campaigns clean and aboveboard.

"And to limit them might be worse than the problem that could be created or the inconvenience caused certain individuals, to limit that, with greater harm than the harm that would be caused by someone losing their right to privacy."

Bill Franklin sagged at the sound of Doumar's words. The wait for the final decision would be long and tedious, and Bill Franklin was no longer optimistic.

In between, he was going to have something worse to worry about.

Someone threatened to kill him again.

Chapter Twenty-six

"Tell Him He's a Dead Man"

"Tell him he's a dead man"
Anonymous Caller

The Surf Rider restaurant is on a street corner in Virginia Beach, just a few blocks off the Oceanfront, but far enough back to be avoided by tourists. The regulars are local people; performers who are in town for shows at nearby clubs often eat there before or after their performance.

Only someone who knew Bill Franklin — or his schedule — would know to call there.

Tim Cunningham, the cook who was working that night, was new on the job. When he answered the phone, the caller asked if Bill Franklin had come in yet.

"I don't even know who Bill Franklin is," Cunningham told the man.

"You better check with Stan Bennett, then, and have him get Franklin to the phone."

Bennett, the restaurant's owner, wasn't in either.

Cunningham called out to Jim Heatwole, the manager.

"Is there someone named Bill Franklin here?"

"No," Heatwole said. "He hasn't come in yet."

Cunningham told the caller that Franklin definitely wasn't there.

"Then give him this message," the caller said. "Tell him he's a dead man."

Cunningham immediately called Stan Bennett at home. Bennett, a former Virginia Beach police officer and close friend of Franklin, was sufficiently bothered that he called the police department before trying to track Bill Franklin down. By the time Franklin got to the restaurant, a police report had already been filed and an additional report had been taken by a uniformed officer from the Second Precinct.

"Those bastards!" Franklin hollered when he heard what had happened. "Can't I even get a meal in peace and quiet in this town?"

Summer came on, lazy and sweltering. Bill Franklin was drinking more, sleeping fitfully, and waiting for Judge Doumar's decision. He hadn't gone to the gym for months; his weight ballooned to nearly 260 pounds.

One afternoon in the middle of June, Franklin was being interviewed at his office by John Sherwood, the former *Virginian-Pilot and Ledger-Star* reporter who had written the first articles on Operation Seagull in 1985 and who was now working for *Port Folio*, a regional weekly magazine. Franklin was going to be the magazine's cover story at the end of July.

The two men had been talking for about an hour when Franklin suddenly ran out of breath.

"Excuse me," he said hurriedly, feeling as if he couldn't quite get enough oxygen. "I have to go to the bathroom."

He splashed cold water on his face and leaned against the bathroom sink, feeling foolish. He took several deep breaths and returned to his office.

When he returned, Sherwood picked up his questions where they had left off, talking about the upcoming decision by the FEC.

Suddenly, Bill Franklin stood up.

"The interview is over," he announced. He walked out of the room, made his way to an upstairs office, and collapsed into a chair, gasping for breath, sweating and shaking cold.

His blood pressure had shot up to a worrisome 220 over 122. The doctor told him what he already knew: if he didn't slow down, lose 50 pounds, and stop smoking, he was going to die. The episode, the doctor said, was caused by excessive emotional pressure and prolonged fatigue. If Franklin continued to burn his candle on both ends, it was going to burn right out.

Bill Franklin was sufficiently scared that he began a reformation. He took a daily blood pressure pill; he went on a diet; he returned to Wareing's Gym, the Oceanfront sweat shop where he labored now under the scrutiny of celebrity.

On July 6, 1989, his blood pressure soared again as he was propelled into total outrage.

The Robb for Senate committee had filed yet another addendum to the original background statement in their complaint to the FEC. This, their third, named names and made accusations that had Bill Franklin positively spinning in fury.

Franklin's clients, the addendum said, were Dr. Lewis Williams and "at least the following individuals." They named Joe Canada, a former Virginia state senator, who had lost to Robb in the 1977 race for lieutenant governor; Canada's wife, Sandy, who had been Tidewater Finance Coordinator for [Paul] Trible for Governor, and a former employee in Trible's Senate office and the Virginia Republican Party; and Alan Fuentes, president of Computer Dynamics, Inc. and a supporter of Paul Trible.

The addendum also accused Joe Elton, Executive Director of the Virginia Republican Party, of having frequent contact with Henry Hudson, the United States Attorney who had spearheaded the grand jury investigation into the Beach drug scene. Rumors concerning Robb, originating with Donald Huffman, the chairman of the Virginia Republican Party, were allegedly passed to Hudson by Elton on Huffman's behalf.

When the grand jury concluded its investigation in May 1988, the complaint said, Robb's foes could no longer utilize the resources of the U.S. Attorney's office and decided to hire Franklin.

The remainder of the background statement outlined alleged dates and locations of meetings between Dr. Williams, Franklin, and Canada, as well as numerous telephone calls between Republican party officers and Franklin and Williams.

When he received his copy of the addendum, Bill Franklin went into a sputtering rage. Some of his closest friends had now been drawn into the fray and, as anyone who knows him will tell you, you can take Franklin on one to one, but don't malign his friends or family.

None of the charges was true. To prove how absurd the Democrats' claims were, Franklin pointed out that one of the alleged meetings between Williams, Canada and Franklin, said to be held in "Franklin's Virginia Beach office" was said to have taken place on January 25 or 26, 1989.

At that time, Bill Franklin was in Roanoke Rapids, N.C., meeting with retired detective Harry House, a graduate of Franklin's Virginia School of Polygraph.

And Franklin never even had an office in Virginia Beach. During the summer flurry of newspaper coverage in which Dr. Lewis Williams was alleged to be Bill Franklin's client, Williams steadfastly denied that he had anything to do with the investigation.

"Why did I lie to the reporters? That's a tough one," Williams said later. "After all that had happened to Bill Franklin, to tell you the truth, I was afraid for my life. I had five children and three grandchildren and a wife to worry about. "It was never my intention to make my name known in this," he added. "I never imagined what would come from all this."

When the *Port Folio* cover story on Bill Franklin appeared on July 25, Franklin's phone started to ring again. The calls were from people throughout Hampton Roads, supporting him in his investigation of Chuck Robb. They told him, too, to stick to his guns about not naming his client.

In spite of the public support, a day after the *Port Folio* story appeared, on July 26, 1989, Judge Doumar ruled in favor of the FEC.

"It is ordered and adjudged that William Franklin a/k/a Billy A. Franklin is to provide to the Federal Election Commission, in writing, full and complete answers to the extent of his knowledge. . . ."

Bill Franklin had 75 days to comply with the order or appeal it.

He decided to fight on.

Chapter Twenty-seven

The Titties of a Sacred Cow

*"By the time the FEC started on me I felt I had
hold of the titties of a sacred cow that was dragging
me through the brambles, and I couldn't let go or
she'd run over me."*

Billy Franklin

The Fourth Circuit Court of Appeals rejected Buster
O'Brien's appeal on Bill Franklin's behalf.

"The Appeals Court didn't even give us a chance to
submit a brief or case law or anything on this," O'Brien
complained to a reporter. "They just handed down this
order saying it's over. I'm absolutely, utterly amazed; I
think this enormously expands the jurisdiction of the FEC
and just opens a vast chasm of potential abuse. I wish we
could have taken this to the [U.S.] Supreme Court, but
that gets to be extraordinarily expensive. Plus Billy's had
a lot of pressure on him. We thought we were right and
we stood up for principle for a long time. But the principle
became too costly."

Franklin was characteristically colorful when he
described his feelings to the same reporter. "By the time
the FEC started on me I felt I had hold of the titties of a
sacred cow that was dragging me through the brambles,
and I couldn't let go or she'd run over me."

As fall came on again, Bill Franklin was up against the
most difficult decision of his life. The first nine months
of 1989 had exhausted him, depleted his resources,
ruined his health. He had three options.

He could go to jail for contempt of court.

He could appeal the decision to the United States
Supreme Court.

He could tell the Federal Election Commission the
name of his client.

Jail, he knew, would be the most romantic. It would be a clear public statement of his idealism, principles in practice. It would also be foolhardy. Who would run his business in his absence? Who would support his family?

Appealing the court's decision would be time consuming at the least, exorbitant in terms of financial cost at best. And there was no guarantee that they would win, no guarantee that it would not, somewhere down the road, turn out the same way again. He met with Dr. Williams.

"It's over," Franklin said. "They've nailed me."

Williams had never imagined, a year and a half earlier, that it would come to this. He told Franklin once again the same thing he had said throughout the process:

"Do your best, but do what you have to do."

Williams, one of the area's leading obstetricians and once the Republican nominee for Congress in the 3rd District, says now that what he felt on that day was resignation. He had feared the notoriety both personally and professionally, feeling as protective of his patients as he does for his family.

"Once the judge issued his decision, there was nothing we could do," he says with a deep sigh. "Bill had no other choice really but to tell them what they wanted to know."

On October 2, 1989, Billy A. Franklin responded to the Order of the Court. He named Dr. Lewis H. Williams as his client and stated that he had been retained as both an attorney and a private investigator to "determine the truth or falsity concerning rumors surrounding former Governor Charles Robb with regard to his drug usage, his association with known drug dealers, his involvement with prostitutes and other females and his association with convicted felons." He was also retained, he added, to "give my legal opinion regarding whether or not the former governor was guilty of any criminal misconduct and whether or not the employer would be liable for civil damages if this information was published in a book about Virginia politics." In February 1990, Dr. Lewis Williams was called to testify before the Federal Election Commission. Both Williams and his attorney were sworn, under oath, not to reveal any questions that were asked or answers that were given during his testimony.

By the time winter settled over Virginia Beach in 1989, Bill Franklin had almost forgiven himself for disclosing the name of a client, something he had never done before and could not have imagined that he would ever be driven to do.

He was appalled at the power the FEC had been able to wield, especially after a year had passed since the election in which Robb had been such an overwhelming winner. Franklin was even angrier when Robb's administrative assistant, David McCloud, told a reporter that the Robb camp didn't care when the FEC reached a final decision or how long it took.

"I realize it's a long process," McCloud said, "but we are determined to pursue it until it is resolved, if it takes two more years, or three, or four, or five — whatever it takes."

Whatever it takes. Franklin remembered those words as his own when he'd thought about continuing his investigation of Chuck Robb. As much as he wanted to do that, he was on his own now financially; every hour he invested in the Robb investigation was an hour taken away from a paying client. In his answer to the FEC, he estimated that, in addition to the $12,500 he had been paid by Dr. Williams, he was owed more than $100,000. That figure easily represents more than 1,000 hours or, calculated at $100 an hour, more than 100 days. On his own.

And although Franklin Security Systems was beginning to show signs of regaining ground, he needed all the income he could get to recoup from the previous year.

Things were picking up so much, in fact, that he had hired a new employee, Ricky Chaplain.

And, unbeknownst to him, the new year was about to turn the tide in Bill Franklin's favor.

Chapter Twenty-eight

Eyewitness

"No one has ever put me in the same room where drugs were being used."
Charles S. Robb, The Washington Post,
September 23, 1988

Ricky Chaplain's family was one of the original ones in Virginia Beach; they easily traced their lineage back to 1635. Ricky's great grandmother, Gussie Chaplain, owned hundreds of acres of land, the value of which would increase dramatically as the city grew. During the 1940's, Gussie Chaplain sold a portion of the land she owned to the government. Where the Chaplain family children once picked strawberries, multi-million dollar jets now land at Oceana Naval Air Station.

There was plenty of land left over, of course. On the 60 acres the family owned between Virginia Beach Boulevard and Norfolk Avenue, they created a trailer park. Value: $10 million. During the 1960's, when Ricky Chaplain was a kid, the family started buying hotels on the oceanfront.

When he was growing up, Ricky Chaplain was required to work and work hard. His grandfather, Wilson Chaplain, was a no-nonsense taskmaster and a firm believer in the value of hard work, especially for family members. He drove the young boy hard. When Ricky came home from school he'd be sent to one of the hotels to paint beams and sweep porches. He often worked until 10 or 11 at night. During the summers, he worked as a bellhop.

Wilson Chaplain was a tough boss but he was not ungrateful. Now and then — Ricky says you couldn't quite ever tell exactly when it was going to happen — grand-daddy would go into town, which is what Beach people call anything that isn't the Beach, and he'd come back with a couple of presents for the boy who worked so hard.

Wilson Chaplain never bought just a Cadillac Eldorado for the young man; he'd get him a pick-up truck to go along with it. The Chaplain family fights like other families have picnics. A few of them will take on a crowd in a five on one donnybrook with the odds against them; no one blinks an eye and they usually come out on top. Now and then, they kick it up among themselves as well.

When Ricky was asked to leave First Colonial High School in 1980 — the fighting had gotten to be just too much for everyone — he bounced around for a while. First he went into the used car business, but he could only handle that enterprise for three months.

"Hey, even I couldn't screw people over that badly," he says.

Next it was a wrecker service and then in 1983 he bought a piece of land on 19th Street in Virginia Beach to build his dream come true, the Pavilion Athletic Club.

At 32, Ricky Chaplain is a bull of an over-grown boy. Big and beefy, with an 18-inch neck and a southern accent as thick as the gold bracelet on his wrist.

By the winter of 1989, Ricky Chaplain had sold his club, kicked cocaine cold turkey on his own, completed the course for private investigators at Thomas Nelson Community College in Newport News and set his sights on the career he wanted.

Bill Franklin had had a nodding acquaintance with Ricky Chaplain for years. They saw one another around the beach hangouts and they both worked out at Wareing's Gym. Ricky Chaplain came to Bill Franklin looking for a job in December 1989. Since business was finally picking up, Bill Franklin hired him.

Ricky Chaplain had been working for Franklin Security Systems for a little more than a month when he came to Bill Franklin in January 1990 looking uncharacteristically serious.

"I need to talk to you about something," Chaplain said, flinging himself into one of the leather chairs across from Franklin's desk.

"What's on your mind, son?"

"I should have come to you before this. But, you know, I was afraid and I didn't know what to do and it's all been so confusin'. So I talked to my Momma last night, talked it over with her, and she said I should go ahead and talk to you. Tell you what I have to say."

"You can say it, Ricky. Whatever it is."

"I snorted coke with him."

"Who?"

"Chuck Robb. Chuck fuckin' Robb. The governor."

For nearly two years, the concentric circles had grown smaller and smaller as Bill Franklin worked his way toward the middle. For all the second-hand stories, for all the as-told-to's, he had not been able to bring forth a person who could — or would — say unequivocally on the record that he, or she, had personally been present when Robb snorted cocaine.

And now right in front of him, in his own office, sat Ricky Chaplain, ready — and willing — to talk.

"I want to turn the tape recorder on, Ricky. That OK with you?" Franklin asked.

"You bet. Let's do it."

The wall that had seemed impenetrable to Bill Franklin for so long was about to crumble.

Chapter Twenty-nine

Tootin' Coke With Chuck

*"He put his head down to the table, stuck the pen
in his nose. . . put his face down there. . .and when
his face came up those two lines were gone."*
Ricky Chaplain, January 1990

This is Ricky Chaplain's story:
By April 1984 the Pavilion Athletic Club was awash in
pretty people, money and cocaine. There was a sign over
the bar from a movie Ricky loved. The sign said: THE
WORLD IS YOURS.

It seemed to Ricky Chaplain that spring as if the world
was, indeed, his. And he was on top of it.

He felt, he says, like Elvis Presley.

He had money in his pocket — lots of money. The club
did $6,000 a night; he'd toss it on a table when he got
home in the early hours of the morning.

Brenda, the woman he'd loved since he was 13 and with
whom he lived, had just given birth to their daughter.

He had, until that time, refused the cocaine that had
been offered to him. "I just didn't want to mess with that
shit," he says.

It was heartbreak, Chaplain says, heartbreak pure and
simple that drove him to cocaine.

"I came home and heard Brenda talkin' to her
boyfriend on the phone," he says, his voice catching a little
even after all this time. "I realized she was screwin' this
other guy!"

Ricky Chaplain's relationship with cocaine began.

He moved to the penthouse of one of the family's
hotels. He had all the women, drugs, money and local
infamy he could possibly want.

He rode around in a black Excalibur and he had
bodyguards, two men each named David who were distin-

guished from one another because one was Uzi Dave and the other was One-Arm Dave. The names were self-explanatory.

The first time Chuck Robb came to the club it was May 1984 and he was with Bruce Thompson, Gene Schmidt and Marty Pallazio. "I was so impressed that the governor was in my club I could hardly stand myself," Chaplain says.

Chaplain watched as the four men went into the club's private office with Chaplain's partner, Willie Shipp.

Robb came back in June 1984 with Gene Schmidt. Ricky was in the office by himself.

"Gene asked me if I did cocaine, and I had just started doing a little bit right then so I said yeah, so we all snorted a line."

"Whose coke was it?" Franklin asked.

"It was Gene Schmidt's."

Schmidt laid the cocaine out on a typewriter tray that slid in and out of the desk, so that if anyone came in it could be easily concealed. The men used a white, pull-apart ballpoint pen with its innards removed to snort the cocaine.

"I snorted two lines. . .about an inch, or inch and a half long," Chaplain said. "And then Gino did it. Gene Schmidt. . .and then Chuck Robb snorted one. He put his head down to the table, stuck the pen in his nose. . .put his face down there. . .and when his face came up those two lines were gone."

When the men left the office, Chaplain said, two men he believed to be state troopers in civilian clothes were standing outside the door.

There were three more occasions during that summer of 1984 when Chuck Robb snorted cocaine with Ricky Chaplain. The second time, they were again joined by Gene Schmidt. The third time, it was Robb, Bruce Thompson and Chaplain.

The fourth and final time took place around Christmas 1984, at a huge gala party thrown for the staffs of a number of Beach restaurants. Among the guests were Thompson, Schmidt, Pallazio, the Dunnington brothers,

U.S. Senator Paul Trible, state Senator Peter Babalas, and other dignitaries.

After escorting an inebriated guest to his Cadillac, Chaplain explained, "We went into the office and snorted cocaine."

"With who?" Franklin asked.

"With Ricky and Chuck Robb."

"You and Ricky Dunnington and Chuck Robb?"

"Yeah."

"Whose cocaine was it?" Franklin asked.

"It was Ricky Dunnington's."

"What did you think?" Franklin asked him a few minutes later.

"Damn, we got a hell of a governor. I thought. . .you know what I thought to myself? God damn, I's (sic) lucky to have the governor of Virginia my friend. At least if I get into trouble, he's got to help me out a little bit, 'cause he was the governor."

Chaplain estimated that in addition to the times he was present, Robb went into the office with Schmidt, Pallazio and Thompson another 20 times between April and December 1984.

Chaplain said that he had no illusions about his connection with the governor.

"The only reason I got in that group is because that one night that Gene and Governor Robb were there. They wanted to go in that office and snort cocaine and I was in there. The only reason I did was they asked me, you know, did I snort coke, and I said yeah and we locked the door and we did a couple of lines. That's how I got in there was 'cause they wanted to get in that office and snort it 'cause that's the safest place to do it."

In talking about Robb's consumption of cocaine on individual occasions, Chaplain said, "He done as much as eight lines."

"That's a lot of stuff," Franklin said.

"No, it ain't. Not when you're rolling. Eight lines is like nothing. And drinking too at the same time."

"What did you think when you read in the paper where he said that he wouldn't know cocaine if he saw it?" Franklin asked.

"I laughed," Chaplain said, laughing again in remembrance. "I couldn't believe it."

Ricky Chaplain has successfully taken a polygraph test to verify his statements.

Chapter Thirty

Calling the Blind Man's Bluff

"Well again, I've got to tell you I don't know that I would recognize cocaine if I saw it."

Senator Charles Robb,
The Virginian Pilot and The Ledger-Star,
August 28, 1988

"His [Robb's] only flaw was his vanity, which wouldn't allow him to don glasses, despite his failing eyesight."

Regardie's Magazine, October 1990

Months later, Ricky Chaplain's stories were confirmed by another one of the men who was familiar with the Pavilion Athletic Club and who had snorted cocaine with Chuck Robb. The man came voluntarily to talk with Bill Franklin, but insisted on anonymity to protect his family.

He had graduated from a Virginia Beach high school in the mid-1960's and, like so many of the young men of his generation who still believed in the American dream, he went to Vietnam because he thought it was his duty. He came home, wiser about the realities of war, and well decorated.

By 1983, the man was heavily into cocaine. He snorted it and he smoked it, enhancing the high but also enhancing the damage. The destruction from his cocaine habit was so bad that his nasal septum was completely eaten away. He could, he told Franklin, pass a pen back and forth through the hole in the cartilage that had been destroyed. In spite of his drug habit, he kept himself in good physical condition and was known at the gyms in town.

Bruce Thompson introduced the man to Governor Charles Robb at the Pavilion Athletic Club in the summer of 1984. Thompson was no stranger to him; the two had used cocaine together on previous occasions.

The first time the man met Robb, he ushered Thompson, Robb and a third man into the office at the club after Thompson asked if he and Robb could use it. He understood, he said, that they wanted to do cocaine in there because "usually when people asked to use the office, you could bet they're not going to write a letter home."

Since the opening of the club, he had used cocaine in the office with many of the customers, including Thompson, Ray Parsons, Gene Schmidt, Paul Van Auken, Ricky Haycox, and Ricky and Bobby Dunnington.

The man told Franklin that he watched as Thompson took a bag out of his pocket and laid several lines of cocaine on the desk, chopping them up carefully as he did so. Franklin's witness left the three alone and went to the men's room. When he returned, the man who accompanied Robb and Thompson opened the door to the office to leave. Inside, Robb and Thompson were clearly visible. And they were snorting cocaine.

"Bruce Thompson was sucking it up," the man told Franklin, "and then I saw Charles Robb's head go down to the desk and he breathed one up too."

The men were using a gutted Bic pen as a straw. They called it a "do-one pen" because with good-sized lines of an inch and a half to two inches long, they put half a line up each nostril. "You can," he said, "only do one."

His reaction when he saw the governor snorting cocaine, he said, was that "I thought I better get my ass out of there." The next time Bruce Thompson brought Chuck Robb to the club, they didn't even stop to buy a drink before making a bee-line to the office. Bruce asked if the pen was in there. After assuring them that it was, the man remembered to tell them that the new Bic pen had a tiny air hole in the side.

"Be sure to put your finger over the hole," he told them. "It will be easier to snort through."

Once again, he watched Governor Robb, Bic pen in hand and finger over the air hole, put his head down toward the cocaine. "He was either going to take a nap with his head on the desk. . .or he was going to snort a line of cocaine," he said. Being in the tiny room with the governor snorting coke made him nervous, so he departed each time the snorting started. "Me and my nervous ass," he said with a laugh, "got out of there." After they were finished, Robb and Thompson usually left an extra line on the desk as a sort of "thank you" for the use of the office.

On the occasions that Robb visited the club, he was accompanied by a man dressed in a sport coat and slacks who flashed a badge and announced himself as "Security." After Robb and Thompson had made their way to the office, the security man stationed himself at the front door of the club.

Bruce Thompson used the man who spoke with Franklin not only for his hideaway but as a pipeline for drugs. On one occasion, Thompson said that he had some women and Chuck Robb and a few other friends at his house at Croatan and needed a quarter of an ounce of cocaine. He referred Thompson to Steve Arcese, another habitue of the scene.

On another occasion when Robb was at the club, a young woman stepped out of the crowd with a camera just as Robb was coming out of the office with Thompson. Apparently excited at seeing the governor, the young woman snapped a photo of him. In an instant, the man who had identified himself as "Security" leapt toward her and knocked the camera out of her hand. The camera shattered on the floor as Robb strode by, wordless.

By the time the man talked with Bill Franklin in 1990, he had been off cocaine since 1988, and with the exception of an occasional beer, used no drugs or alcohol.

He came off cocaine, he said, when his mother overheard someone in a grocery store talking about him. The horror of his mother finding out what his life had become, combined with the physical damage he had suffered, made him realize that he had to straighten out his life.

Like Ricky Chaplain and others who came forward during Franklin's investigation, the man looked back on 1984 and 1985 with a sense of outrage. Never denying their own wrong-doings, they nonetheless retain a sense of anger at Chuck Robb's public lies about his drug use in their midst.

Bill Franklin felt triumphant. It had taken almost two years, but the eyewitness account of Ricky Chaplain had finally cracked the protective circle that had surrounded Robb for so long.

Nonetheless, Franklin believed that if there were two people willing to come forward, there had to be others.

As he had so many times during the previous two years, he put the word out every place he went that he was interested in talking to people about Robb.

Two more eyewitnesses came forward in February.

Chapter Thirty-one

High on Harborfest

"It was just, hey, he's got a boat, come on over here, bang a bottle of. . .I think it was a bottle of beer or whatever it may have been."
Chuck Robb, on his relationship
with Ricky and Bobby Dunnington,
The Virginian-Pilot and The Ledger-Star,
August 28, 1988

Frank Gore was in the plumbing and heating business. By the time he came to talk to Bill Franklin on February 5, 1990, he had been out of prison for less than a year, after serving nine months for possession of cocaine and attempting to distribute the drug. Before he was arrested, he had been the manager at an Oceanfront restaurant and right in the middle of the cocaine scene.

Why, Bill Franklin wondered, was Gore willing to talk about this now?

"I think people need to know what really happened back at that time," he said. "He was the governor; he was representing the state. And things should come out in the open about the whole thing. The whole truth should come out."

Frank Gore met Chuck Robb for the first time at Harborfest, an annual event in Norfolk, in 1986. Ricky Dunnington had called Gore and asked for an ounce of cocaine for a party they were going to have on their boat, the "Sea Raven." At that time, Gore was known to most of the heavy cocaine users at Virginia Beach as a reliable dealer.

He took the cocaine, with a street value of $1,600, to the dock at the Norfolk waterfront where hundreds of yachts and sailboats tie up every year for the three-day festival. He met the Dunnington brothers around four o'clock in the afternoon and they took him aboard the boat, down into the cabin.

Five people were already there: Hampton Wolf, who worked for Gore as a drug dealer; the 20-year-old daughter of a prominent businessman and restaurateur; a Filipino girl who was the manager of the Raven at the time; another girl whom Frank Gore had never seen before, and Chuck Robb, the governor of Virginia. All three of the women were topless.

Bobby Dunnington tested the cocaine for purity by cooking it up, adding a little water in a tube and warming it with a small torch. What Frank Gore had brought them turned out to be 90 percent pure.

After paying Gore, Dunnington smoked the free base, the powerful residue from the cooked down cocaine, that remained. Bobby Dunnington asked if Gore realized who the other man was, indicating Robb.

Gore said he did.

Dunnington assured him that everything was cool and that he need not be worried. The governor, he said, was just one of the boys.

Bobby Dunnington took some cocaine out and laid it on the table. Using a straw, he did a couple of lines. Chuck Robb was next.

"Where did Robb do the line?" Franklin asked.

"Right there," Gore said, "right on the table there."

"Along with everybody else?"

"Yeah. They had a little kitchen and had a table that came out."

"Did he do just one line?"

"Two," Gore said. "Two lines."

How, Franklin wanted to know, had Gore felt about snorting cocaine with the governor?

"I felt like, Governor Robb is doing coke, why shouldn't I do it? You know, why shouldn't I be selling it?"

"Was there any question that he knew that they bought the coke from you?" Franklin asked.

●

"No, because he saw me come aboard with it," Gore replied. "As a matter of fact, there were a couple of state troopers on the dock."

"On the dock?" Franklin asked, surprised. "What were they doing? How did you know they were state troopers?"

"Bobby told me," he said. "He said 'You don't have to worry about anything.'"

Gore told Bill Franklin that as he prepared to leave the boat, he noticed that Robb was involved with the Filipino girl. Robb was kissing and fondling the young woman's bare breasts.

After Frank Gore was arrested on drug charges and convicted in April 1988, he wrote a letter to Robb, who had returned to private law practice by that time, asking for help with parole. "I figured he could help," Gore explained. "I figured, you know, we snorted cocaine together and he knew that I brought the cocaine to the boat. I figured he could pass it down and I could get an early parole."

"Did he?" Franklin asked.

"No, he didn't. I never got an answer back from the letter."

The woman who came with Frank Gore to meet Bill Franklin was Gore's girlfriend, Susan Styron Rixey. A woman who had been her roommate in June 1986 had been on the "Sea Raven" that same day. The roommate told Rixey that Robb had been on the boat, but Rixey said she found it hard to believe at first.

"She told me that Chuck Robb was on the boat. . . .she said they had the bottoms on. . . .the girl came home with a T-shirt on from the Raven because her titties were so sunburned she couldn't wear the top of her suit."

"Did she say that she had seen Chuck Robb?" Franklin asked.

"Chuck Robb. Yes."

The roommate told Rixey that Robb was snorting lines with the rest of them in the cabin of the "Sea Raven" while thousands of people milled around outside, celebrating Harborfest.

Rixey, who had been heavily involved with cocaine herself, had been clean for nearly a year before meeting with Franklin. She talked about the deep and overwhelming paranoia that cocaine causes and how some people in the crowd had been affected by it. Bobby Dunnington's cocaine habit was no secret. He had been freebasing for years — they jokingly called him a "base face" — and employees at the Raven even used the drug during operating hours right behind the bar.

Along with his cocaine habit, Bobby Dunnington developed a love of electronic equipment that would keep him on top of everything that was going on. More than one person had talked to Bill Franklin about Dunnington's police scanner, telephone recorder that indicated the number of the calling party, and the video camera he set up so he could see anyone who was coming or going at his Oceanfront condominium.

Gore and Rixey had more than one confrontation with Dunnington and his paranoia before they got out of the drug scene. Dunnington owed Gore a small amount of money for a drug buy and, although he kept promising to pay whenever they were able to get hold of him, more often than not he didn't answer his phone or his door.

According to the people who knew him, Dunnington stayed inside his condo for increasing lengths of time as his cocaine addiction worsened. His brother, Ricky, they said, was trying to figure out a way to help him but seemed powerless to stop the decline of his twin.

Bobby Dunnington seemed to be one more victim of what had started out as just a bunch of boys with a lot of money having some fun and reaping the spoils of success.

Rixey spoke as emphatically as anyone Bill Franklin had talked to when he asked why she had agreed to speak with him on the record about Robb's cocaine use.

It was, she said, Robb's hypocrisy that was bothering her.

"That makes me sick! The fact that he was doing lines and he's getting lines from the same people we were, and that my boyfriend served time on the same stuff he was doing," she said.

"When you're in the public eye you're setting an example for thousands and thousands of other people," she added. "If you're telling children 'Just Say No' when you say yes to everything that comes your way, whether it be pussy or cocaine. . . .I don't get it."

Chapter Thirty-two

Courtney Gets a Civics Lesson

"What the hell is the governor doing here with these people, and myself snorting cocaine, drinking and carrying on. . .and he's supposed to be a person that people look up to with respect and authority and look to for guidance."

Courtney Cromwell, March 1990

Bill Franklin felt vindicated. The new year had brought him the eye witness confirmation of Robb's drug use that he had sought. He had believed for so long that it was true; now he could prove it.

The idea of writing a book of his own began to stir in his mind. He suspected there were more people who might be willing to talk to him to add to the first hand knowledge or complete the picture of Robb's activities now that the wall was crumbling. There were.

Courtney Kane Cromwell was the quintessential beach girl. Tall, attractive and well-built, she was 17 in 1982 and was at the heart of the young girls on the verge of womanhood who found acceptance, fun and excitement in the midst of wealthy men. With a toss of her hair, she admits that she was a spoiled little rich brat in a city that seemed to breed a lot of them, as if they were a genetic blueprint of one another. Long hair, long legs, the best clothes, good cars, pocket money, and an eye for action.

Courtney Cromwell attended the prestigious, Oceanfront Star of the Sea Catholic School for the elementary grades and then Virginia Beach Junior High. She moved, briefly, to Cape Hatteras, North Carolina, where she graduated from high school, but she returned at once to the Beach.

And like so many of the other young women who were part of the Beach's in-crowd during the early 1980's, she'd grown up on the Oceanfront and had access to all the best bars and clubs because she was pretty and fun to have around. And she liked to party. It didn't seem to matter to the proprietors that she was under the legal age to be in these places; she was part of the crowd.

Cromwell's name had surfaced over and over during the course of Bill Franklin's investigation. At last, he located her. She agreed to meet with him at his home on March 11, 1990.

In the summer of 1982, Courtney had been 17 and running in the fast crowd. Invitations came for parties at Bruce Thompson's Croatan house. There she was introduced to the rest of the guys: Chuck Robb, Gene Schmidt and Marty Pallazio.

It was in Marty Pallazio's house, in fact, in the kitchen upstairs, that she watched Chuck Robb snort cocaine for the first time.

She believed that the cocaine had been provided by Bruce Thompson since he was the one who laid the lines of coke out on the kitchen counter for the others to snort through $100 bills. She estimated that there had been a quarter of an ounce of cocaine, enough, she said, to keep six people happy all night. Cromwell wasn't doing cocaine herself, at least not then. Like the other girls, she drank a lot and smoked marijuana, but the cocaine didn't come until later.

The parties she went to were the ones that everyone had always talked about. Gorgeous homes, furnished expensively, where dozens of men and women laughed and talked. As in any other society, there were distinct strata: everyone knew who the wealthiest ones were. They were the ones who owned the houses, and you could tell their women by the way that they were always dressed to kill. Jewelry abounded. If you weren't snow-blinded by the cocaine, the glitter of gold and diamonds could do you in. Beneath them were the ones who were well enough off, but who probably had to work for their money. They couldn't quite afford to shop at the chic boutiques, but slipped instead into the better department stores — Thalhimer's was well-liked enough — to find off-the-rack copies that looked good.

Cromwell and her girlfriends populated yet another strata, the one to which the party girls have been relegated throughout history. As long as they were up for a good time and good to look at, they were encouraged to be around.

So through the years 1982 to 1984, Courtney Cromwell was invited to lots of parties. They were her way of life.

And Chuck Robb was a part of the parties. Seeing him there and watching him use cocaine in customized kitchens became not only not unusual, but almost mundane. In spite of the straight-arrow image that he has managed to project in public for more than two decades, the private glimpses of young girls like Cromwell tell a different story.

She estimated that between 1982 and 1984 she saw Robb snort cocaine on a dozen different occasions.

"You watched him with a straw in his nose?" Franklin asked.

"Right. And a straw in his hand," she said.

Franklin asked her what she had thought when, as a teenager, she had watched the head of the state she lived in snort cocaine. She remembered thinking, she said, "What the hell is the governor doing here with these people, and myself, snorting cocaine, drinking and carrying on. . .and he's supposed to be a person that people look up to with respect and authority and look to for guidance."

After listening to similar recitations during the previous two years, it came as no surprise to Bill Franklin when Courtney Cromwell said that cocaine was openly used at the parties by nearly everyone in attendance and that the parties often reached an orgiastic pitch.

Being at the parties was exciting. "I was young, it was dumb, it was exciting. . . .It was like a challenge. It was like 'what are we doing here? we're not supposed to be here.'"

"How do you feel about Bruce Thompson saying he never does drugs?" Franklin asked her, referring to interviews Thompson had done with newspaper reporters.

"I know for a fact that's bullshit," she said.

"Have you ever seen him do drugs?"

"Many times."

"How about Gene Schmidt?"

"Yeah, well God himself and all the devils in the world have seen him doing it."

"How about Marty Pallazio?"

"Yes."

"How about the Dunnington brothers?"

"Yes. Ricky especially. . .always had a bag of cocaine." She had some strong thoughts on the fall-out from the drug probe, she told Franklin.

"I think it's very peculiar given the situation with several different people being convicted and are locked up and currently serving prison sentences, that Ricky and Bobby Dunnington — Ricky especially — has never been convicted by the Drug Enforcement Agents, state and local police, or anything else for that matter. "I think," she added, "someone is looking out for them." One of Cromwell's favorite places to party in 1982 was Summer's, the same club where John Bass tended bar when Bruce Thompson asked him to provide cocaine and women for a party for Chuck Robb.

It was at Summer's, Cromwell said, that she was approached by Bruce Thompson. He asked her to have sex with Robb.

"Bruce Thompson approached you to do what?" Franklin asked her, startled.

"To sleep with Governor Robb."

"You're talking about screwing Robb?" Franklin asked.

"Yes," she replied quietly. "He told me that the price would be right."

Courtney Cromwell said that she declined the offer.

"Did that bother Bruce Thompson?" Franklin asked. "What did he say?"

"He said 'Are you sure you don't want to do that?'"

She told him she was absolutely sure.

There were other girls, however, some of whom Cromwell described as "young, young girls" who were more willing to party openly with Robb and the others.

At one party, she said, a girl with long curly hair was "wild."

"What do you mean 'wild'?" Franklin asked.

"I mean dancing on the tables, taking her clothes off, the whole nine yards. I thought, I've got to get out of here."

"What was Robb doing?" Franklin asked.

"Loving it," Cromwell said.

"What do you mean 'loving it'?"

"He acted like a dog in heat," she said with disgust.

In talking about her background, Cromwell readily admitted to Franklin that she had been arrested in 1986 for possession with the intent to distribute marijuana. She received a 15-year suspended sentence and supervised probation.

She had come to talk to Franklin, she said, because she too was tired of the duplicity of Robb's public persona contrasted with his private behavior.

"I just think that what I know, what others know, about Chuck Robb should be told."

She paused briefly, then went on.

"I think everything he stands for is a lie."

It was late when Courtney Cromwell left Bill Franklin, well after midnight. He went to check on Smokey, his big old black dog. The dog had cancer and had been getting chemotherapy. Franklin knew as soon as he stepped into the utility room that the dog had died, and he leaned against the door jamb. He hoped that there was a dog heaven. He sure cared a hell of a lot more about that dog than he did about some people, particularly men in public office who lie.

Courtney Kane Cromwell has successfully taken a polygraph test to verify her statements.

Chapter Thirty-three

April, 1990

"I firmly believe that any man's finest hour, his greatest fulfillment to all he holds dear, is that moment when he has worked his heart out on a good cause and lies on the field of battle, victorious."
                                                                Vince Lombardi

As spring approached, the earth came to life again in Virginia Beach. The sun had shifted, lingering longer each day. The sand and soil began to warm. Tree tips fattened with leaves-to-be.

Bill Franklin thought back over the past two years. In April of 1988, a month before Dr. Williams first contacted him, he could not have imagined — could never have dreamed — the nightmare that awaited him, nor the sense of triumph he would feel in the end.

He would not have said, two years before, that he could be called naive. Politics and politicians, he had always known, were a special breed. Like the rich of whom F. Scott Fitzgerald had spoken, they are, in many ways, different from you and me. But two years earlier, Bill Franklin had believed that there was fundamental decency in high places and that the people who put their hand on a Bible, swearing to uphold the Constitution of a state or a country, would be fundamentally decent.

Two years later, he had come to believe differently. And he had come to experience, first hand, the damage that can be done, to individuals and to the greater good, by power.

Power was no stranger to him. He had used it often. And yet the type of power he had come up against during his investigation of Chuck Robb, an investigation he had undertaken in the belief that he would absolve the man, had shown him what power could do. He saw with a clarity that unsettled him deep in his belly how power and corruption looped together at so many levels, weaving groups of people together in a web of lies, self-protection and self-serving gains.

But in the end, he had made it through. Hadn't quit his investigation, hadn't lost his business or his family, hadn't sold out and hadn't been killed.

He had the answer to the most important question of all. He had discovered that he was tough enough.

Now, he wondered: where would he go with what he had learned? It was not enough that he knew the truth. He believed that this truth needed to be shared.

He had two years of his life invested in this investigation — hell, it had become his life — and over $100,000 of his time. All along the way, as the investigation had become mired down, as he had seen how difficult it could be to get at the truth, when he had confronted and been blocked by fear and the power it can generate, the idea of writing a book had played around the edges of his mind.

Now that he had what he had sought for so long, now that he could name people and places and dates — the threats on his life, invading his sanctuary, his home; the bribes that insulted his integrity; the witnesses: Ricky Chaplain, Courtney Cromwell, Frank Gore, Susan Styron Rixey; the FEC power that had been wielded against him. He could not find a single reason to delay further.

He decided to write the book, taking it upon himself to expose Robb. The media and law enforcement officials seemed unable — or unwilling — to bring the true story of Robb's drug use where it belonged: to the public. Franklin knew that he was the one person who had boxes of notes, hours of tapes and transcripts, documentation and testimony that no one had ever been able to get before, linking Chuck Robb to cocaine use. And he believed that he had a debt to pay, an obligation to fulfill to the men and women who had been brave enough to come forward with the truth they knew, who were willing to risk so much by speaking it.

Chapter Thirty-four

Another Long, Hot Summer

"The [Washington] Post could be the key. It could lead the rest of the press by exonerating Robb or by burying him. Robb may have to clear his name himself."
Regardie's Magazine, October 1990

With another goal clearly in his sights, Bill Franklin felt exhilarated and almost tireless. He continued his investigation even as the writing of the book began.

Word filtered out gradually into the community that the project was under way and Bill Franklin's phone began to ring again.

Many people came forward willingly. They offered insights into the personalities of the Virginia Beach people who were closest to Robb; they explained situations that had seemed murky. It is illegal, for instance, for local police to investigate any elected official without the approval of the attorney general. When the governor is among the people the local police would like to investigate, it becomes difficult to get that approval from another member of the executive branch.

Fear, they said, pervaded the community during the federal grand jury proceedings. It was fear of retribution, personally or through business, that kept people from talking to Rose Ellen O'Connor and it was that fear, in the beginning, that had made Franklin's job so difficult.

Fear. Fear was pervasive throughout the Oceanfront as Franklin continued his investigation, unrelenting. Like the prostitutes, Frankie and Jamie, who turned to Preston

Berry when they felt trapped between the party scene and the police, there were others who lived in fear of their involvement. Although the events were four, five, six, even seven years old, the memories lingered. And as Robb rose to political power — and as the newspapers carried the stories of the death threats to Bill Franklin and his defeat by the Federal Election Commission — the possibility of retribution seemed to grow, at least in the minds of the people who remembered.

People who had once bragged about having Robb in their life now lashed out in counter-attack. Confronted with the allegation that he said on numerous occasions that he had snorted cocaine with Robb, Don Kern, out of prison and proclaiming himself an innocent victim of a DEA witch-hunt, growled to a reporter, "If Bill Franklin prints that, I'll kill the bald-headed motherfucker."

It was no wonder, Franklin thought, that he'd had so much trouble getting people to talk to him. Robb's friends and acquaintances were dangerous.

Arrogance played no small role in how things were at Virginia Beach between those years 1982 to 1987. Some of the men who talked with Franklin expressed regret not at what had happened, not illegal drugs being used or street hookers being paid to entertain wealthy men, but at the fact that they had been caught. Those interviews were the most difficult to endure. Time, it turned out, was the critical factor. As Robb's star continued to rise on the political horizon, many of the people he left behind in Virginia Beach felt ripped off. Many also felt betrayed by his lies. Robb's duplicity seemed to increase in importance to his former friends after he became a senator and now that he may become a presidential candidate. Some people talked with Franklin willingly at first, then backed off. Tai Collins, the beauty pageant winner who had dated Robb while he was governor, was one of those people.

A meeting between Franklin and Collins was arranged by a mutual friend at the friend's home on Tuesday, May 29, 1990. Collins, wearing a light summer dress, was even prettier than Franklin had expected the former Miss Virginia-USA to be.

She seemed not the least bit nervous and spoke calmly and openly with him.

Yes, she had met Chuck Robb at the dedication of Waterside and had dated him in Virginia Beach, she said. And yes, she had seen a lot of cocaine used at parties they attended together but she had never used cocaine herself nor had she seen Robb use it. Yes, Bruce Thompson had been the intermediary contact for the two of them much of the time and yes, Robb had come to visit her in New York on one occasion, she told Franklin.

Her estranged husband, in fact, was attempting to use the adverse newspaper publicity about her former relationship with Robb in their on-going divorce proceedings.

Lynda Robb, she said, had been unhappy about their relationship and had "raised hell" with Robb about it.

Tai Collins said that she considered Robb "not very smart." Collins said that Rose Ellen O'Connor's story had "bugged her," and the placement of her photograph — the only woman — in the midst of ten men who had been involved in the drug probe seemed to unfairly imply that she, too, had been involved in the investigation.

It was during the summer of 1988, she told Franklin, when there was so much negative publicity and the senatorial campaign was heating up that Hunton and Williams, Robb's law firm, had taken a deposition from her. The questions they asked her under oath, she said, were extremely personal.

Several times during the conversation, Collins asked Franklin about the exact nature of the information he had concerning Robb. He told her nothing.

At the end of their two-hour talk, Collins agreed to meet with Franklin and his writer two nights later, Thursday, May 31, at Franklin's home.

She left a message at Franklin's home on the afternoon of the 31st, saying that she needed to reschedule the meeting and would be in touch with him to do so.

He waited four days. Bill Franklin finally caught up with her on her car phone. She said that she could not have another meeting with him.

A mutual friend later told Franklin that the day after Franklin's meeting with Collins, Chuck Robb's top aide, David McCloud, came to town and convinced Collins that it would not be in her best interests to have any further discussions with Franklin.

The power and the fear had intervened once again.

Some people would still not talk to him at all. Bruce Thompson was contacted through his attorney and declined to be interviewed. Although several requests were made, neither of the Dunnington brothers came forward either.

The dangers of releasing the volatile information he had were clear to Bill Franklin. It was conceivable that the Robb camp would stop at almost nothing to forestall publication. But he knew that somewhere, sometime, somehow, he would have to let someone outside of his writer see just what he really had.

By the middle of the summer, with enough work completed on the first draft to begin discussions with publishers, Franklin took his manuscript to Hampton Roads Publishing Co., Inc., where publishers Bob Friedman and Frank DeMarco had the first look at it.

Friedman had been a principal at Donning Publishers in Virginia Beach, a successful regional publishing company, for 16 years before striking out on his own; De-Marco had just left *The Virginian-Pilot* as an editorial writer.

Not unexpectedly, the two men were stunned at the information Franklin had uncovered and confirmed about Robb. They feared, though, that publishers would shy away from the potential law suits the material could generate.

They suggested that Franklin take his story directly to the public first, using the mass media as a catapult for the saga. At first, Franklin grappled with that idea. Releasing his information to newspapers could mean that, although the truth would emerge once and for all, he would never regain his own extensive investment of time and money. In the end, the public's need to know outweighed concern for his personal benefit, although he still retained the hope that he would someday be compensated for his efforts.

Friedman, who had agreed to act as agent at this point, and DeMarco initially contacted the hometown newspaper, *The Virginian-Pilot and The Ledger-Star*. DeMarco, who made the call to a senior editor in Norfolk, said that he offered the manuscript in its entirety but also suggested that Franklin would be amenable to some kind of compensation.

Franklin's offer was rejected out of hand by the newspaper without any further discussion or negotiation. The same offer was made to *The Washington Post*. They expressed immediate interest and Don Baker, a senior and broadly experienced reporter for the major national paper, arrived on a July afternoon at the Hampton Roads Publishing offices. After discussions between Billy Franklin, his agents, and Baker, the reporter contacted his Washington office to tender the details of Franklin's offer. Very quickly, messages passed from one level of editor to another, reaching *The Washington Post* pinnacle, Ben Bradlee, executive editor.

Bradlee's message back to his reporter was that *The Washington Post* would not pay any money for the manuscript, but would commit its full faith and resources to investigating the Robb affair if the material in Franklin's manuscript seemed substantive.

In a scene comically antithetical to the seriousness of the entire undertaking and Bill Franklin's two years in this intense political drama, Don Baker received and immersed himself in the manuscript while lounging in a floating chair bobbing on the surface of Billy Franklin's pool. He wore a pair of borrowed swim trunks. The reporter thumbed through the then-200 page manuscript between exclamations of surprise and also confirmation.

Baker had worked this same story for many years and immediately recognized the extent, the depth, and the sweat of Franklin's effort. Within days, *The Washington Post* teamed Baker with a top investigative reporter, Tom Heath, for a full-time, full-blown, thorough investigation of the Robb matter.

Within a week, the reporters were ensconced in an Oceanfront apartment.

Word of the now-heightened investigation and the forthcoming book leaked further into journalistic circles.

Alicia Mundy, the reporter for *Regardie's* Magazine who was implicated by the Federal Election Commission in the original complaint against Franklin, was already in the process of working on an article about Chuck Robb and the forced resignation of Henry Hudson, the United States Attorney who led the grand jury investigations that implicated him in the Beach cocaine scene. Mundy arrived in Virginia Beach to interview Bill Franklin as soon as she heard about his book. A former newspaper reporter in Arlington, Va., Mundy had been watching the on-going Robb scenario for many years.

Suddenly, things began to go topsy-turvy. When eyewitness Frank Gore was contacted by *The Washington Post*, he confirmed everything he had told Bill Franklin up to the point of actually seeing Robb snort cocaine, but he backed off there. After a flurry of long distance phone calls, the truth emerged: Gore had been frightened when he realized that everything was going to be made public at last, he told Franklin. He once again confirmed for Franklin that he had, indeed, watched Chuck Robb snort cocaine aboard the "Sea Raven."

Gore was not the only person who was frightened. Many people reacted in a similar fashion to the presence of the newspaper reporters and the realization that all would soon be known.

"I'll talk to you," they told Franklin, "but I'm not talking to *The Washington Post*."

Eventually, many of them did. Once the wall had been broken through, once the dam had started to leak, there was no way to stop it.

Which is not to say that the Robb camp didn't try. After interviewing Franklin, Alicia Mundy contacted Robb's chief of staff, David McCloud, who had been the initiator of the FEC complaints. McCloud seemed not to believe that Franklin's book existed. Mundy indicated that she has seen the book (she had read one chapter, but not the entire manuscript) and that Franklin had a number of witnesses to Robb's dalliances.

McCloud asked, "These women. . .did they say they had sex or intercourse?"

In subsequent conversations with Franklin, Mundy revealed that she had confirmation from both the Robb camp and John Warner's camp that Henry Hudson would not be reappointed because of his handling of Robb and the grand jury cocaine sessions in Virginia Beach.

She also told Franklin of McCloud's strategy for seeking an FEC injunction against him for releasing the book to *The Washington Post* and to *Regardie's*.

Within days of being contacted by Mundy, McCloud fired off yet another salvo to the FEC, just as he had told Mundy he would. This seven-page, single-spaced missive was a windfall of whining. The same man who had, little more than a year earlier, said boldly that they were willing to wait ". . .if it takes two more years, or three, or four, or five — whatever it takes" in reference to the Federal Election Commission's final report was, on August 28, 1990, stamping his foot like a recalcitrant child. "In the 24 months since I filed that complaint," he wrote, "the Commission has neither completed this proceeding nor provided any information to us on whether or when it will reach a decision in this case."

On and on he went, recapping the case, adding new allegations, frantically urging the FEC to act on what McCloud called "Franklin's utter contempt for the authority of the Commission" by citing him for breaching confidentiality and therefore preventing the publication of his book.

If the issue was "utter contempt for authority," McCloud bore more than his own share of guilt. He sent copies of the entire package of information to members of the press before mailing it to the Federal Election Commission or Bill Franklin. In the press packet was a copy of a 1988 letter, on Hunton & Williams letterhead, from George Stoddard, former Robb press secretary, to United States Attorney Henry Hudson, confirming the details of a press conference that would announce the conclusion of the investigation into drug trafficking in the Hampton Roads area and would clear Robb of any wrongdoing in connection with drug activities.

A press "feeding frenzy" began on September 22, 1990, when the Fairfax *Journal* and the Richmond *News Leader* ran the information provided by David McCloud. Two days later, on September 24, Bill Franklin released his client's name to *The Washington Post*.

The first story confirming Dr. Lewis Williams' identity appeared in the *Post* on September 25, 1990.

By Wednesday, September 26, every newspaper between Virginia Beach and Washington, D.C., with the exception of *The Virginian-Pilot* and *The Ledger-Star*, ran coverage of the breaking story. The Norfolk newspapers, dragging their heels and playing catch-up with the state's other newspapers to report the story that was breaking in their own back yard, quoted the state Republican party leader, Donald W. Huffman, as saying that he had contributed about $300 to help pay Bill Franklin and that he had attended a private discussion early in 1988 with other party officials in reference to hiring a detective to look into Robb's social life.

Days later, editor William Wood penned an editorial sneering at Franklin's investigation, the impending article in *Regardie's*, and the renewed public interest in Senator Chuck Robb's days and nights in Virginia Beach.

With a tone that pooh-poohed any clamoring by the electorate for further information about a top government official, Wood wrote, "There's little question that Mr. Robb used poor judgement by socializing with some people who, as it turned out, had unsavory reputations. But that was five years ago." He urged that scrutiny be shifted from Robb as governor to Robb as senator.

Throughout the community, the newspapers' readers felt insulted by both the tone and the content of Wood's editorial. Sources at the newspapers indicated that Wood had been advised against such a "Don't pay any attention to the man behind the curtain" stance.

At the end of September, Alicia Mundy's cover story for *Regardie's* magazine, entitled "The Resurrection of Chuck Robb," hit the newsstands. A long time Robb-watcher, Mundy traced Robb's life and political career to what seems to be its inevitable conclusion: a run for the Presidency.

A sidebar about Bill Franklin's investigation and forthcoming book was spread out across the *Regardie's* article's two interior pages. Its title: "Chuck's Chappa-quidick?"

Within days of the *Regardie's* article, Bill Franklin's sources began to stir with unsettling news: Bobby Watson, Chuck Robb's Virginia director and Senate campaign staffer, was on his way to town.

Chapter Thirty-five

Intimidation

"I realize it's a long process, but we are determined to pursue it until it is resolved, if it takes two more years, or three, or four, or five – whatever it takes."
David McCloud

An informed source with political connections told Bill Franklin that Bobby Watson was coming to Virginia Beach with a multi-purpose plan: to assess the allegations about Robb, to disprove the allegations about Robb, and to ascertain exactly what information Franklin had.

Two days later at a wedding, a long-time friend of Franklin's with connections to the Democratic party took Franklin aside to warn him that Watson was coming in to lean on Franklin's witnesses, to do what he could to discredit Franklin, and to shore up the support of the local Democrats.

The woman also told Franklin that an offer would be forthcoming to buy the rights to his manuscripts, but not with publication in mind.

Chuck Robb was livid, she said, and Franklin's safety could be in jeopardy. She had overheard a conversation in which Robb said that he would kill Franklin himself if he thought he could get away with it.

Bill Franklin was worried about the turn events were taking. The first thing he did was to contact his witnesses to warn them. But he couldn't find Courtney Cromwell.

Robert Eringer, a literary agent in Washington, D.C., contacted Franklin after seeing the article in *Regardie's*. Eringer, like others who had seen the manuscript, believed that it lacked national appeal and would be better suited to a magazine piece or a television segment, with a biography of Bill Franklin coming out later. He offered to contact CBS' "60 Minutes" and gave Franklin the name of a producer there.

Bob Friedman, still acting as Franklin's agent for the book, sent a copy to a New York publisher. The response from the canyons of Manhattan was "Who's Chuck Robb?"

After several days, Courtney Cromwell re-emerged in Virginia Beach, much to Franklin's relief. Concerned over a parole violation she might have committed, Cromwell had gone to Deborah Rawls, the attorney who had represented her on a marijuana charge, for help and advice. In an effort to explain her situation as clearly as possible, Courtney told Rawls about her involvement with Robb and her testimony to Franklin.

"She was scared to death," Rawls said, "and she came to me." What Cromwell did not know, then, was that she had just talked to a direct pipeline to the Robb camp: Rawls is married to Billy Hutchens, a Robb staff member and close friend of Bobby Watson, Robb's Virginia director and Senate campaign staffer. Upon her return, Courtney Cromwell was confronted by Bobby Watson and Billy Hutchens while she was at work at the Days Inn at the Oceanfront. They wanted to talk to her about what she had told Bill Franklin. She said she wouldn't tell them anything. "If you do this, you'll be sorry for the rest of your life," Watson told her menacingly. And just to be sure she knew who he was, he left his business card with her. Hutchens stood by, glowering.

The following day, the two men made a point to walk by the big window at the front of the hotel. They slowed, looked in, caught Cromwell's eye. And gave her what she remembered as "evil stares."

Angered more than scared now, Courtney met again with *The Washington Post* reporters to confirm that Robb's representatives had confronted her.

Within days of their visit to Cromwell, the duo of Watson and Hutchens turned into a trio; David McCloud joined the men. They made their way through circles of key, prominent local Democrats, one of whom was former detective, now-Sheriff and long-time Franklin friend, Frank Drew.

"Billy Franklin is one tough son-of-a-bitch," he told them. "I wouldn't want him investigating me."

Franklin was the toughest investigator he'd known in all his years in law enforcement, Drew added.

During the meeting, Watson told Drew that Robb and his supporters intended to use all the legal powers that a senator possesses to destroy Franklin.

"The big mistake you people made," Drew told the men before they parted, "was threatening him."

Just as Franklin had been forewarned, he was approached at the end of October about selling his manuscript to suppress it. A prominent Virginia Beach businessman, long known, respected, and considered a friend by Franklin, asked if they could meet at a local restaurant. When the men sat down together, it became clear that the topic under discussion was to be Franklin's manuscript and its contents.

The man told Franklin that local Democrats had asked him to speak to Franklin on their behalf, for the good of the state, the local party and its members.

Franklin outlined what evidence he had against Robb; the man was shocked.

He then asked Franklin if he had a publisher for the book yet. Franklin said that he did not.

"Would you be interested in selling the manuscript?" the man asked. "And how much would you want for it?"

"I'd consider any legitimate offer," Franklin told him. Franklin was intentionally cagey in his response. When he had been warned that an offer would be made to take the manuscript off his hands, Franklin was advised by attorney Buster O'Brien that to name a firm price could be construed as extortion or blackmail at some future time.

Franklin explained to the man that he had already forgiven about $100,000 in fees and expenses unpaid by Dr. Williams. What he didn't add was that by the time of their conversation, Franklin had an additional $150,000 invested in the investigation of Chuck Robb, bringing his own investment to about a quarter of a million dollars.

The man told Franklin that he was concerned for Franklin and his family, Buster O'Brien and his family, and even, he said, his own family.

And he said that he'd like to meet with both Bill Franklin and Buster O'Brien together the next time. A date and time for the meeting was arranged.

When the three men sat down together, the tone of the meeting was far different from the first one. Franklin and O'Brien listened intently as the man explained that he had been led by the Democrats to believe that members of his own family appeared in Franklin's book in an unfavorable light. Franklin explained that that was not true.

Franklin also explained his intent to publish the manuscript himself and said that he was anticipating coverage from *The Washington Post*. The man shook his head negatively.

"It's not going to happen," he told Franklin.

"What?" Franklin asked.

"I have it on good authority that the *Post* has been taken care of," the man said.

Franklin was astounded. What he was being told seemed impossible — wasn't it *The Washington Post* that was so proud to have broken the Watergate story? — but after all that had happened in this investigation, there was nothing that he would rule out. The past two and a half years of his life had been so filled with knock out, gut wrenching developments that the idea of a major national newspaper being "taken care of" seemed just one more blow.

The man went on to say that he wanted time to meet with a highly placed Democratic official and then to meet with Franklin once more.

The man never called again.

So far, most of the word that had reached Bill Franklin had come true: Robb's people had come to town to lean on witnesses, and an offer for the manuscript had been tendered. Now Franklin worried that this most recent information about *The Washington Post* was true as well.

He confronted *Post* reporter Don Baker, who vehemently denied that anything had happened to kill the story he was working on. But as October ended and a new month began, the story, originally scheduled for late September, still had not run.

Chapter Thirty-six

Media Madness

"I think it is the press' job to inform people and let them make judgements. . . .I don't think it's up to us to withhold. . .to use our opinions on what the public should and shouldn't know. I think we have to tell the public everything reasonable that we know."
Kathryn Graham, CEO, The Washington Post

On the night of Sunday, November 11, Bill Franklin received a call at his home from Marion Goldin, a senior producer for NBC. It was late; he was tired. He told her to call him the next day. The following morning, Goldin was on the phone once again. She explained her background — she had been a producer at CBS' "60 Minutes" for fourteen years — and that she had seen the article in *Regardie's* about Franklin's book. She was planning to come to Virginia Beach the following week and requested a meeting with Franklin. He agreed.

Franklin met with Goldin for the first time on Monday, November 19, at the Oceanfront. She said that she hoped to do a segment on Robb for NBC's new program, "Expose," which would make its debut early in January, 1991. After preliminary discussions, Franklin allowed her to take the manuscript and read it that afternoon. They planned to meet at Franklin's house that evening.

When Marion Goldin arrived, she was in for a surprise. Actually, two surprises: Ricky Chaplain and Courtney Cromwell were there to talk with her. After listening to their stories, Goldin arranged to videotape them the following day.

Things moved into high gear on Tuesday, November 20. The NBC film crew arrived. They shot Ricky Chaplain in front of the Pavilion Athletic Club and Courtney Cromwell, who finagled Goldin into springing for a $100 hair-do, at Croatan.

Goldin spent most of the following day with Franklin and on the telephone in her motel room, contacting people named in the manuscript. Goldin and Franklin met for a final discussion at Norfolk International Airport. During that talk, Goldin bemoaned the fact that she was working alone and could use some help on this story.

At the same time, out on the west coast, former *Virginian-Pilot and The Ledger-Star* reporter Rose Ellen O'-Connor, who had gone to work for The Los Angeles *Times*, was longing to return east to be closer to her ailing father. Word got to O'Connor that there might be work with NBC.

Within days, NBC hired O'Connor as a consultant to the network for a two-month period. She would work exclusively on the story she had come to know so well two years earlier.

In her excitement, O'Connor called her old friend and *Virginian-Pilot and The Ledger-Star* editor and former boss, Dennis Hartig, to tell him everything that was going on.

Resounding silence emanated from Washington, D.C. The long-awaited *Post* story still had not run. Don Baker was in touch almost daily with Franklin and his book team. But like the journalistic equivalent of "The check is in the mail," the only thing he could say was "We're working on it."

Fearing that he would be treated by NBC as he now believed he was by the *Post*, Franklin requested a written commitment from Marion Goldin that NBC intended to air the information he had provided. He received her letter on November 27.

The following week, the Richmond *News Leader* ran a story about NBC's involvement with the Robb story after obtaining a copy of the letter from Goldin. A similar story appeared the following day in the Richmond *Times-Dispatch*. Although copies of the letter had apparently been sent to newspapers throughout the state, no other paper carried the story. And despite the fact that editor Dennis

Hartig had heard all the latest developments directly from Rose Ellen O'Connor, *The Virginian-Pilot and The Ledger-Star* continued to ignore an about-to-be-national news story.

On December 12, word came at last from the *Post*. They needed photos for the story, which was now scheduled to run on Sunday, December 16. Franklin scurried around to provide what he could, and waited.

Sunday morning came. There was no story in *The Washington Post*.

Franklin was livid; his fear was that some force or power greater than that of the American press had, in fact, intervened. Two days later, the *Post* sent photographer Mary Lou Foy, formerly with the Miami *Herald*, to take pictures of Bill Franklin, Ricky Chaplain and Courtney Cromwell. The story, it seemed, might be alive and well after all.

In the meantime, NBC's Goldin and O'Connor were hard at work, shaking up the Virginia Beach community. People who had long hoped that the Robb affair was part of their past cringed when they answered the telephone only to discover that it was television calling.

Whatever impact Bill Franklin's initial investigation and the subsequent questions asked by the *Post's* Baker and Heath might have had on witnesses to Robb's partying and cocaine use, the introduction of the electronic medium generated a new level of nervousness and paranoia. For television is a seductive medium in American life. If it's on TV, it must be real; if it's on TV, it must be important.

"We are an event simply by our presence," one local television producer said while talking about how cameras create a sort of Heisenberg principle of their own: the mere act of observing a phenomenon changes it.

Telephones jangled between the people who were receiving requests from NBC for interviews. Strategies were discussed. Rumors flew among those who had been, and in some cases still were, close to Robb as to who had already talked, on camera, to NBC.

The holidays were fast approaching. It seemed doubtful that the *Post* would run such a damaging story so close to Christmas, but bets were on that the story would run on Sunday, December 30. That is until Don Baker, who had once kept in touch so regularly and who had seemed so open, now returned fewer phone calls. There was no story on the last Sunday of the year. Two weeks later, Don Baker called Franklin. There would be no *Washington Post* story about the Robb affair, Baker said with tremendous remorse. His editors, he said, had spiked the story, were withholding it for publication because it lacked what they considered to be witnesses sufficiently credible to accuse a sitting United States Senator of drug use.

Franklin was reeling; meanwhile his sources reported that the media rumor mill was churning. One story was that Lady Bird Johnson, the former first lady, had intervened with her dear friend and *Washington Post* publisher, Kathryn Graham. The rumor was that Mrs. Johnson, whose friendship with Kathryn Graham has been well-documented, pleaded with her to suspend publication of the sordid story about her son-in-law. It was said that Kathryn Graham informed the paper's editors that *The Washington Post* would not be the first to tell the world about Chuck Robb's unseemly and criminal behavior. However, Graham was reported to have told the editors, once the story broke, the *Post* would be compelled to report the facts. A further rumor alleged collusion between the *Post* and NBC news, which had agreed to take the responsibility for breaking the story, leaving the *Post* blameless in the eyes of the Johnson family.

There were other rumors as well, including that the *Post's* top editors didn't believe that Ricky Chaplain and Courtney Cromwell were strong enough witnesses, first because Chaplain had worked part-time for Franklin Security Systems, and second, because Cromwell had a criminal record. Although the reporters had good, solid interviews with women who had had affairs with Robb, they weren't going to go with the sex story alone, but might resurrect the material at a later date if Robb decided to become a presidential candidate.

Franklin was mad as hell; he felt like a naive country girl who had come to the big city and given away her favors. He despaired of having looked to the media for assistance; he rued that he had held up his own book on their behalf.

Franklin was also sickened by the turn events had taken at the *Post*. He had only recently watched a videotape of a 1987 program on ethics, the media and politics, shown on public broadcasting stations and used as a resource by media students, in which Kathryn Graham, faced with a hypothetical situation almost identical to the one the *Post* now faced, had said, "I think it is the press' job to inform people and let them make judgements. . .I don't think it's up to us to withhold. . .to use our opinions on what the public should and shouldn't know. I think we have to tell the public everything reasonable that we know."

Bill Franklin knew that he would wait no longer. His resolve to self-publish was strengthened.

The turn of the year is a lucky time for Bill Franklin. He thought he had all the eyewitnesses to Robb's drug use that he needed but he was about to get another one.

Chapter Thirty-seven

One More Eyewitness

"The Beach is the best."
Charles Robb, while using cocaine in 1984

The final eyewitness who came to Bill Franklin was a blond woman who had turned 37 years old in January 1991 and had been a born-again Christian for almost two years. She was a member of the Rock Church, a large Virginia Beach congregation of fundamentalist Christians. Five years earlier, long before she was saved, she had worked as promotions director for a local radio station and been a member of the Virginia Beach Jaycees from 1985 to 1987.

Unsought, unexpected, she came to Franklin of her own volition early in 1991. She had heard about his investigation of Chuck Robb, and the pressure Franklin was under. She decided to add what she knew to what Franklin already had. When they met at his office in January 1991, he tape recorded the conversation with her permission.

This is her story:

In 1984, the East Coast surfing championships were held at Camp Pendleton, and Governor Robb was invited to attend to give out the awards. He was, he said, going to be in the area anyway and would be happy to put in an appearance.

The radio station for which the woman worked was one of the sponsors of the event, and her job that weekend was to take Governor Robb around the site, to see that his needs were tended to, and to oversee photos taken of him with surfers, Jaycees and political supporters. A Winnebago had been pulled onto a sand dune, right beside the stage, to serve as a home base for the Jaycees. So when the governor needed to go to the bathroom, it was to the Winnebago the woman escorted him.

Entrance to the Winnebago required knowing a secret knock (even she admitted how silly that sounded) known to only a select few. It involved a few raps on the door followed by a scraping of fingernails and then a couple more sharp taps. It was the scraping of the fingernails that made the difference as to whether or not the door would be opened to you.

The woman knew the special knock and she knew the reason for it too: people were using cocaine inside. She'd been in there a couple of times herself during the course of the weekend, doing coke with some of the Jaycees. In fact, she left a vial of her own cocaine on the table inside.

(Snorting cocaine doesn't exactly fit the picture the public has of this civic organization, but the woman told Franklin that it was the reason she left the group in 1987 after belonging for only two years. "They do wondrous things for the beach," she said, "but they don't do it unless there's drugs and alcohol going on. When you're raising money for underprivileged people you don't need to do it in partying until you drop dead.")

A Jaycee member opened the door to the Winnebago and the woman entered with Robb. There was a brief flurry of activity. The Jaycee diverted her attention to the roster of people who had already been entertained in the trailer, telling her to fill it out. At the same time, he was directing the governor to the bathroom.

When the woman sat down at the table to fill out the report, she noticed that the vial of cocaine that had been there when she and Governor Robb walked in was gone. She was aware of it at once, she said, because it was hers.

Before she could ask about it, the other man in the trailer tried to convince her to leave, to take the list of other guests to Bruce Rader, a local sports announcer. Complaining that it was too far to walk all the way over to the stage and back again, she lingered.

Robb emerged from the bathroom after a very short time. "I'm finished," he said to the other man.

The woman told Bill Franklin that she was painfully aware of the fact that Robb had not flushed the toilet.

"I thought to myself 'How tacky!'" she recalled.

She had to use the bathroom herself and noticed that the toilet appeared unused.

When she emerged from the bathroom, the missing vial was back on the table. Empty.

Like any good cocaine user, she was all too aware of how much coke there was, to whom it belonged and exactly what happened to it.

"Where's mine?" she whined to her friend.

"Just take Mr. Robb out and come back," he said abruptly. She complained that it was too far to walk all that way. "Just do it my way," the man told her tersely.

So she did. But at the first opportunity, she returned to the Winnebago without Robb.

She confronted her friend.

"What's going on here?" she demanded.

"You don't need to know," he said.

"Well, that was mine, what was sittin' on the table and he goes in there and he comes back out and it's all gone and you tell me to never mind. . . ."

"OK, wait a minute. I'll fill it back up."

He refilled her vial with cocaine from a bag of his own and then said, "OK, now just forget what you saw here."

Years later, she remembered well her previous feeling of shock.

"I couldn't believe what I had participated in with our governor!"

She told her husband about the incident right after it happened. He gave her a piece of advice: don't ever be the one to directly hand the cocaine to Robb and don't ever take it directly from him.

Only a few hours later, the advice would come in handy. She went to a party in a private home; the cocaine was in a back bedroom so it could be stashed if anyone unexpected came through the front door. The woman estimated that there were about 75 people there, all of whom were doing cocaine at one time or another during the night.

Chuck Robb, who had arrived before she did, was already in the back bedroom.

"We were all gettin' off on the fact that we were doin' it with the governor," she recalled, laughing heartily.

"I mean, we were all goin' 'Hey! This is pretty heavy!'"

The cocaine was laid out on a mirror the length of the bed. "Like choo choo train tracks," she said. "And you just went in and did however much you wanted."

They used a solid gold snorter; she noticed right away that no one passed it from hand to hand. They all laid it down and let someone else pick it up. Just like her husband had warned her to be sure to do.

Ray Parsons, who would hang himself in jail just a few years later, was in charge of providing drugs that night, although Billy O'Dell seemed to be the host for the party.

Robb was accompanied by a man the woman had never seen before, and whom she described as younger than Robb, tall, thin, with brownish hair. Twice during the two hours that she stayed at the party, Robb whispered to the younger man, "Give him some money."

And, following orders, the younger man dug in his pocket and came up with cash for Ray Parsons, who went out and returned with cocaine. Once it was three one-hundred dollar bills; on the second occasion it was a $1,000 bill.

"Who in the world carries that in their pocket?" she remembered thinking.

The role of the younger man seemed to generally be of service to Robb, in addition to paying for the cocaine.

"Getting his drinks, picking lint off of him or just, just touching him," she said, as she described the interaction between the two men.

At the same party, she recalled, two uniformed police officers arrived about 15 minutes after she did. She was about to make her first trip to the bedroom for cocaine when they walked in, hats in hand; she was startled.

Ray Parsons reassured her. "'Be cool, be cool, it's fine,'" he said. "Don't you feel safer that they're here?"

Calmer now, the woman made her way to the bedroom. When she came out, the two officers had changed into civilian clothes. They became part of the party, talked with Robb, and did cocaine. "I felt more protected when they got there," the woman said. "I felt comfortable with them there."

It was a year before she would see Chuck Robb again. In the summer of 1985, the surfing championships were moved to the Oceanfront and the Jaycees used several rooms at an Oceanfront motel as headquarters.

The Sunday in August was marred by torrential rain. Robb arrived in a limousine, accompanied by a blond man the woman described as a "well manicured, very immaculate Robb clone." As Robb was due to be brought to the motel, Jaycee Bob Smith, who was in charge of the championships that year and who was perceived by other members as too straight and untrustworthy of their drug secrets, was hustled out on a make-believe errand. Three male Jaycees, Robb, the man who accompanied him, and the woman were all in the motel room. A small manila envelope bulging with cocaine lay on the dresser beside the door to the bathroom. As he walked by, Robb picked up the envelope and carried it in to the bathroom with him.

When he emerged from the bathroom, he handed the envelope to his friend. The other man laid a pile of bills on the dresser. Smiling, Robb then said, "The Beach is the best." They all knew what he meant and basked in his approval.

"Would you take Mr. Robb back to his limousine?" one of the other Jaycees asked the woman.

She did as she was told.

As she reflected back on those two summers, the woman recalled thinking that "[Robb] was a real cool dude, a pretty happening guy," who was right in there with the rest of them, using drugs.

The only time she worried about being busted when he was around was at the first party in 1984 when the music got so loud that she feared the neighbors would call the police, never suspecting that the governor was there. Like others who had used drugs with Chuck Robb, she said, "I felt very comfortable when he was around."

At Jaycee board meetings, she said, Robb's activities were a source of jokes. "We didn't see him do anything," board members said to one another, tongue in cheek, as they rolled their eyes. "I didn't see anything. Did you see anything?"

"What did you think when you saw in the newspaper that Robb said that he wouldn't recognize cocaine if he saw it?" Bill Franklin asked her.

"I thought it was a joke," she said. "An all-out lie."

Chapter Thirty-eight

Chuck's Chappaquidick

"Faced with a frontal assault on his image, Robb conceded that he'd have been better off at home. 'Can you fault me for enjoying what you would call the beach scene and thinking that I could get away with it?' he asked The Washington Post. Yep."
Regardie's Magazine, October 1990

Nineteen-ninety-one came on mild but wet in Virginia Beach. Bill Franklin had what he had wanted for almost three years: enough eye witnesses to Senator Charles Robb's cocaine use to expose Robb as a sham.

Looking back he remembered his own naivete at the beginning of the investigation, when he thought he would find the rumors that Robb used drugs to be unfounded beach tales. He remembered his disgust at the first stories of Robb's sexual dalliances, and how he eventually became almost enured to their tawdriness. He remembered the pressures that had been brought to bear on him, pressures to which no common man would have access: the grinding FEC proceeding, still unresolved; the Internal Revenue Service's timely audit; the arrival of yet another federal agency, the Army Corps of Engineers, forcing him to relocate a dock that had been standing for more than a decade.

He thought about the death threats that had been made. It seemed as if his entire life had been affected; no part of it was immune from the pressure and prying of Robb and his supporters. He thought about the jeopardy he had put his family into. He wondered how someone else would have fared, someone with fewer financial resources, less tenacity.

He saw the irony in comparing the lives of the people who had come forward to talk with him, to tell the truth about Chuck Robb, compared to the person they were willing to talk about. Ricky Chaplain, Courtney Cromwell, Frank Gore, Susan Styron Rixey, the former Jaycee: not a saint among them. These people were not perfect; these people were not the cream of society, not wealthy, certainly not powerful, and surely not always straight and right and good. But they did not claim to be.

In the end, Bill Franklin saw that it was the truth spoken by people who had made mistakes of their own along the way that would expose Chuck Robb. People who were, at the least, honest. Perhaps *The Washington Post* and *The Virginian-Pilot* and *The Ledger-Star* needed a different type of witness and multiple corroboration to the incidents of Robb's drug use, but these witnesses were good enough for Bill Franklin. These were men and women who were willing to dig deep to find their own integrity and to speak out, to expose themselves to public scrutiny if necessary, in order to stop the lie of Chuck Robb.

Looking back, Bill Franklin saw that what he had was not simply a story of a politician who used cocaine and had affairs with women, but a story of arrogance, power and its misuse, corruption and duplicity. Worse yet, it portrayed Robb's stupidity on a grand scale. It terrified Franklin: the man who had been elected to represent so militarily strategic a state as Virginia in the United States Senate had behaved in ways that made him vulnerable to bribery, corruption and blackmail. Franklin wondered about the unanswered questions too. Would Eddie Garcia have been killed if the plot hadn't been foiled? Would his own life been snuffed if the death threats hadn't been made public? He thought about the allegations from the aborted Operation Seagull and wondered at the questions of Robb's involvement in it, so publicly expressed in the media and still unanswered. Why was it shut down? And why wasn't an investigation undertaken?

He wondered about the men on the state police's Executive Protection Detail. Did they talk among themselves at night about the doors they guarded while the state's highest official snorted coke?

Questions, questions. Bill Franklin knew that he could spend the rest of his life trying to find answers to these questions and the other one, the one that still nagged at him, over and over: what in the name of God had Chuck Robb been thinking of? More frightening still, what if no one had ever told the truth? Bill Franklin knew that there might always be more questions.

He also knew that the time had come to go public with the answers only he had.

Franklin hoped that the long-promised media support would be forthcoming, but he could no longer depend on it. He had waited long enough.

He had decided to publish the book himself and to distribute it through an old fashioned grass roots effort. He had been out there all alone for all this time. He was willing to go the rest of the way alone if he had to.

The final manuscript was ready to go.

With the ever-present threat of law suits and an injunction looming, Bill Franklin knew that the coming weeks would be chaotic and would no doubt throw him into the spotlight once again.

It didn't matter.

He had proven that he was unstoppable, that there was no place for the truth to hide, no matter how hard people tried to conceal it, no matter how much pressure was brought to bear. He had faithfully followed his mother's advice:

"Billy, never go looking for a fight. But if you can't avoid it, don't give one damn inch."

On Wednesday, April 24, word came that the story was approved by top brass at NBC and would run on "Expose" the following Sunday night. The media swung into gear to cover the breaking story; the Robb camp, unable to stop the new wave of attention despite their relentless threats, turned their agenda to a defensive mode. Knowing that the first news stories would be carried on Friday, April 26, they scheduled a press conference for that morning in Richmond.

The weekend was filled with banner headlines and television news stories of Tai Collins' claim to have had an affair with Robb, his presence at parties where drugs were used, and Robb's continued disavowal of any wrongdoing.

When the NBC segment aired, Collins revealed her ten-month affair with Robb to a national audience. On camera, Robb vehemently refuted Collins' story, but admitted to sharing a bottle of champagne with the former beauty queen at the Hotel Pierre in New York City.

In a display of disregard for the work he had done, and despite their promises to give credit to his investigation and book material, NBC omitted Billy Franklin's name from their report.

As we went to press, the print media — with *The Washington Post* in the lead — continued to release details of Billy Franklin's investigation and Robb's activities at Virginia Beach while he was governor. Billy Franklin's friends and supporters, as well as growing number of media representatives, eagerly anticipated the publication of Franklin's book.

And despite a doubting public, the preponderance of evidence against Chuck Robb continued to emerge.

Epilogue

by Billy A. Franklin

Most ordinary citizens would like to believe that honesty, integrity and character are traits that every one should possess inherently. Political hacks, media advisors and the like, whether they're Republican or Democratic, spend millions of dollars attempting to convince voters that their particular candidates possess wonderful characteristics.

It should come as no shock to members of the U.S. Senate or the U.S. House of Representatives that many citizens throughout the country (citizens who vote, work, pay their taxes and obey the law) believe a large conglomeration of thieves, perverts, drug users and liars meets in Washington, D.C.

Voters are bombarded with stories of corruption, perversion, theft, sleaziness and, most of all, arrogance, about their elected officials in Washington. It is said that we get the kind of representation in government that we deserve. What is true is that some Americans believe they have a right to expect — to demand — that those politicians they elect to serve are honest, that they have integrity, moral character and ethics, and they stay drug free. At least they could tell the truth. Americans also believe they have a right to investigate any politician they suspect has abrogated his responsibility to the office he holds and to the citizens he serves.

But, woe to the ordinary citizen who should question the honesty, the integrity, the character, or the ethics of any member of the "Good Old Boy" network.

The problems and pressures I encountered in this investigation are not unique to Virginia or to the city of Virginia Beach. They exist in every state in the union.

My investigation and this book may never make one bit of difference to the character of politicians sent to the House of Representatives or the U.S. Senate from Virginia or, sadly, to the Presidency of the United States. Charles Robb and his kind will still serve in the U.S. Senate, or, even worse, be touted as presidential timber.

One may ask: Why did I, despite threats, political pressure, and economic hardship continue my investigation? I had no other choice. The drug problem that permeates the U.S. is a cancer infecting our nation. At the very least I owe a debt to every police officer who has laid down his life fighting our drug war.

I owe a responsibility to every mother and father who have faced the gut-wrenching problem of drug abuse by their own children. I owe it to those parents who lay awake at night crying for help to end the misery of a problem that they don't understand and can't correct.

I owe every cop and investigative reporter who has been transferred or fired because they dared look into the illegal activities of the rich and powerful. I owe a debt to those damn few politicians who practice what they preach, to their honesty, to their integrity, and to their character. I owe my own parents, my family, my employees and my friends. They kept the faith.

But — after all is said and done — I completed this investigation and book for me, for Billy Austin Franklin.

So many times throughout the course of my investigation I was told that no one really gives a damn whether politicians are honest. I was cautioned by well-meaning and protective friends that I was simply "pissing in the wind." Well, maybe.

But I persisted because I would like to believe that Senator Charles Robb, confronted with the evidence of the truth of his acts, would then apologize to every voter in this state and resign from office.

But then again, it really doesn't make a damn bit of difference to me what Senator Chuck Robb does. What is important to this old fashioned private eye is that I still believe that one man or one woman can make a difference. And, just possibly, when I'm dead and buried, someone will say: "When the chips were down and the pressure was on, he didn't quit. He was man enough to finish what he started. He sure was tough enough."

Billy Franklin
April 1991 ~ Virginia Beach

Billy Franklin was born in Seminole, Oklahoma in 1935. He graduated from the University of San Diego with a B.S. in Business Adminstration. He served as a special agent with U. S. Army Counterintelligence Corp., and in 1961 opened a private investigation agency in Falls Church, Virginia. Mr. Franklin read law, and passed the Virginia Bar Exam, and he has been president of Franklin Security Systems in Virginia Beach since 1963.